I WAS A CIA AGENT IN INDIA

John D. Smith

With Analysis and Background by

Wendell Minnick

Including Analysis on the 1955 Air India Bombing

Copyright © 2015 Wendell Minnick

All rights reserved.

ISBN-10: 1507892403
ISBN-13: 978-1507892404

CONTENTS

Note To Reader	1
I Was A CIA Agent by John D. Smith	2
Target Zhou Enlai	30
Air India Bombing and Zhou Enlai	34
Documents	51
Bibliography	77
Index	84

WENDELL MINNICK

Wendell Minnick (顏文德), B.S., M.A., is an author, commentator, journalist and speaker who has spent two decades covering military and security issues in Asia, including one book on intelligence and over 1,000 articles.

Since 2006, Minnick has served as the Asia Bureau Chief for *Defense News*. From 2000-2006, he was the Taiwan Correspondent for *Jane's Defence Weekly*.

Minnick's first book, *Spies and Provocateurs: A Worldwide Encyclopedia of Persons Conducting Espionage and Covert Action, 1946-1991*, continues to be a benchmark for Cold War research on espionage 20 years after publication. He also produced the *Directory of Foreign Aviation Companies in China: Commercial and Defense* (2014).

Periodicals include *Afghanistan Forum, Air Force Times, Army, Army Times, Asian Profile, Asian Thought and Society, Asia Times, BBC, C4ISR Journal, Chicago South Asia Newsletter, Defense News, Far Eastern Economic Review, International Peacekeeping, Jane's Airport Review, Jane's Asian Infrastructure, Jane's Defence Upgrades, Jane's Defence Weekly, Jane's Intelligence Review, Jane's Missiles and Rockets, Jane's Navy International, Japanese Journal of Religious Studies, Journal of Asian History, Journal of Chinese Religions, Journal of Oriental Studies, Journal of Political and Military Sociology, Journal of Security Administration, Journal of the American Academy of Religion, Marine Corps Times, Military Intelligence, Military Review, Nation Shield, Navy Times, Pacific Affairs, Powerlifting USA, South Asia In Review, Taipei Times, Towson State Journal of International Affairs,* and *The Writer*.

NOTE TO READER

I conducted this research during the early 1990s. It was not an assignment, but was a real obsession over Smith and the 1955 Air India bombing. I traveled to Hong Kong, Taipei, and Washington, DC, to conduct research on the subject with the intention of writing a book. The subject did not generate enough interest with publishing houses, though it did get published as an article in the Hong Kong-based *Far Eastern Economic Review*. When I dug up this material from my file cabinet in early 2015, I realized I had not done anything with it in over 20 years. Today, with print-on-demand options, allowing the information to be readily available for researchers indefinitely and not wilting away in the burrows of a library, I decided to consolidate my old newspaper clips, interviews, and notes as a readable work for the historian.

I WAS A CIA AGENT IN INDIA[1]

No. 5, December 1967
Price: Seventy-five Paise
Printed by the Communist Party of India

PUBLISHER'S NOTE

The brief and incomplete reports in the daily press about the publication of articles by John Smith, former CIA agent, in Moscow's *Literaturnaya Gazeta*[2] have created a great furor and keen anxiety in Indian political circles.

Therefore this pamphlet is brought out so that our people can understand how serious is American and especially CIA interference in the political and social life of our country.

I WAS A CIA AGENT IN INDIA

John D. Smith[3]

I was born[4] in the city of Quincy, Massachusetts, USA. I spent my first seventeen years of

---

[1] This is the original text. It has not been altered and includes all misspellings and grammatical errors. The only difference is that I have included footnotes for background and further explanation. This text is based on the published text by the Communist Party of India, which was compiled from three articles in the Moscow weekly *Literaturnaya Gazeta* in 1967. There are also factual errors about Smith's earlier life that suggest that this propaganda tract was not actually written by Smith, but perhaps by a ghost writer in the Soviet Union. There are also odd spellings, such as the British English style of writing words, such as "neighbour", that indicates Smith did not write this tract.

[2] A weekly cultural and political newspaper published in the former Soviet Union.

[3] The full name is John Discoe Smith. The U.S. State Department Biographic Register does confirm his employment from 1954-59. I filed a written request for information about "John Discoe Smith" in October 1992 with the KGB Archives Department. After the Soviet Union collapsed, KGB files were opened to researchers and historians. I received a phone call on April 27, 1993 from an official assigned to the Russian Embassy in Washington, D.C. "No longer living in the Russian Republic. No such person living in Moscow. No information about John Discoe Smith. No information on his final destiny." Smith's wife claimed he suffered from mental illness, which raises the possibility Smith ended up in a mental institution. See: Grose, Peter, "US Defector in Moscow is Pictured as a Paranoid in Wife's Testimony in Florida Divorce Case," *New York Times* (December 5, 1967, 12). There is some precedence for this. A former employee of the US National Security Agency (NSA), Victor Hamilton, who defected to the Soviet Union in 1962, reappeared in 1992 in a mental institution outside of Moscow under the name of Ingvar Konstantinov, diagnosed with paranoid schizophrenia (Douglas Stanglin, "The Defector Time Forgot," *US News and World Report*, June 15, 1992, 19). Hamilton was a naturalized US citizen from Libya who moved to the US in the 1950s. He changed his name from Hindali to Hamilton. He began working for the NSA in the Middle East section in 1957. He was fired for psychological problems in 1959. In 1963, he defected to the Soviet Union. Then in July 1963, Hamilton wrote a letter to the newspaper *Izvestia* claiming the NSA was intercepting communications between the Middle East and their individual offices in the United Nations in New York. At the time, NSA stated that Hamilton was diagnosed as a paranoid schizophrenic.

[4] Born in 1926. As of 2015, he would be 89, if still alive.

my life there. I was an only child and lived with my mother and step-father. My step-father, who was of Finnish extraction, was named Thomas Kantola. My father was a fine man who was very loving toward me.

When I was seven years old I was sent to the elementary school near my home. We boys studied the usual subjects at school and played football in Mr. Faxon's cow pasture while the cows peacefully cropped grass. I concluded my secondary education at Thayer Academy[5] which was located in the neighbouring town of Braintree.

In 1943 I went to work at the Fore River shipyard where warships were being built. I was a boiler-maker's helper and worked on the aircraft carrier Ticonderoga.[6] I only worked at the shipyard for a few months and left to volunteer for the US Navy. The first months of my naval service were spent at the naval station in Newport, Rhode Island. I attended several naval schools and received a permanent assignment to a special section of Navy Headquarters which was engaged in deciphering enemy codes. My job was very interesting and I enjoyed it very much.

I will always remember the evening when we deciphered a Japanese telegram disclosing the location of five Japanese destroyers. We immediately radioed the information to the Pacific Fleet Headquarters and it wasn't hours before we were informed that all the ships had been sunk. We were very proud of our accomplishment, we the common sailors of America. We were happy and proud of what we had done because we knew that the great people of the Soviet Union were making disproportionally heavy sacrifices toward victory over the common enemy. We were proud that we had managed to contribute in their useful endeavor.

After World War II I continued my education at George Washington University.[7]

I first entered Room 1110 in the Department of State Building in Washington, DC, in October 1950. A tall energetic looking man, with a bald suntanned head, powerful neck and severe weatherbeaten face, rose from his desk and strode across the room to meet me. Ralph Anderson had been my commanding officer in the Navy. He slapped my shoulders affectionately – we hadn't seen each other for several years. After the war Ralph Anderson left the Navy to become an adviser in the Cipher Section of the United States Department of State.

"I'm delighted to see you, John. Sit down and tell me what I can do for you?" He pushed the desk lamp which obstructed his view of me aside and was all attention.

"Commander, I'm looking for a job. It seems education isn't enough to keep the larder full these days. You know I'm an old timer in code – is there any chance of working for State?"

Ralph looked at me piercingly.

---

[5] Thayer Academy responded to my request for information on Smith. It is clear that Smith did not attend this school before joining the US Navy, but after the war. In a letter, included later in this analysis in the Documents section, dated April 10, 1992, from the Thayer Academy archivist: "He was not a regular student at Thayer, but attended the Veterans School which was a special school set up by the Academy after World War II to assist returning students to earn college entrance credits. He did attend Quincy High School before working at the Fore River Shipyard and joining the US Navy, and then took advantage of the opportunity to earn college entrance credits at the Veterans School." Fore River Shipyard was owned by the General Dynamics Corporation located on the Weymouth Fore River in Quincy, Massachusetts. It closed in 1986.

[6] USS Ticonderoga (CV-14) was commissioned in May 1944 and saw serious combat in the Pacific against Japanese forces on the Philippines, Hong Kong, and Japan.

[7] GWU is located in Washington, DC, near the US State Department. It is not clear if Smith attended GWU, but from the end of World War II in 1945 till he went to the US State Department in 1950 would have been plenty of time to secure a degree.

"Say, John, how would you like to go to South Africa? Our embassy in Pretoria needs a code man," he told me.

That was the beginning of my employment in the American State Department. The department of the executive branch of the United States government in charge of relations with foreign countries, the department charged with making friends with other countries and peoples.

At that time I wasn't particularly interested in politics. But as fate would have it, my country's policies gradually had a greater and greater influence on my life. Abroad I had the opportunity to see the United States government in action – its suppression of nations and policy that would bring the world to the brink of catastrophe. Its diabolical policy provides jobs for thousands of the Central Intelligence Agency's and Military Intelligence's employees. Eventually this policy will destroy millions of innocent people.

I know from experience that many of my countrymen are not aware of the dangerous policy being carried out by their government. Many Americans have been brainwashed and cannot or are unwilling to perceive the truth. Woe to the doubting Thomases that question the "American way of life"! They will be plagued with threatening letters, anonymous telephone calls, ridiculed and blackmailed by the papers, be tagged as "Reds"[8] and eventually fired from their jobs. Today's heretics are constantly subjected to loyalty tests, their phones tapped, their homes bugged, their mail read and their friends and neighbours questioned. I experienced these methods of police control of one's thoughts and, believe me, it is intolerable.

On the other hand, many people are unable to understand what is really taking place in the world, who is pulling the strings, and what it may eventually lead to. This is of course a complicated problem. One must have extensive knowledge, reliable information sources concerning events, and the ability to use your head. At one time I naively and sincerely believed that the Central Intelligence Agency existed for the sole purpose of protecting the interests of American citizens. That is why I readily agreed to become an intelligence agent when the job was offered to me. I had a rude awakening when I discovered that the functions of the CIA had nothing to do with the interests of the American people. It is involved in a senseless, dangerous business that is certainly not in the interests of the man in the street.

I worked in many American embassies for a number of years. Among them were the embassies in Ceylon [Sri Lanka], South Africa, Saudi Arabia, Pakistan, Afghanistan, and India. I learned how the United States foreign policy was carried out. After all, there are no secrets that can be hidden from the code clerks.[9] They know more than most people. Many of my friends with whom I cooperated were employed by the CIA.

They made no attempt to conceal information from me. Besides, my former wife, Mary London Smith, was also on the staff of the CIA. Thus I had an opportunity to analyze matters in detail.

---

[8] Common name used to describe Communists during the era.

[9] During the Cold War, the US State Department and CIA would use the same code clerk to transmit encrypted messages in US embassies. It was not practical to have a different code clerk for each US embassy. According to CIA veteran officer, Victor Marchetti, and a former US State Department intelligence analyst, John Marks, the CIA had complete control of code rooms in US embassies. The CIA communications clerks handle almost all classified cables between US embassy and Washington, DC. It was not cost efficient or practical to have a separate code room for both the US State Department and CIA. A senior CIA communications specialist is normally assigned to the administrative section of the US State Department to handle both communications. See: Marchetti, Victor, and John D. Marks, *The CIA and the Cult of Intelligence* (NY: Laurel Books, 1980), 173.

Discovery

Once I understood how matters really stood, I found them unacceptable. I became critical of the policy of my government. This was soon discovered by the United States secret police. My wife's attitude toward me was one of suspicion. I was placed under surveillance and I felt greatly oppressed. I was forced to resign from my government job and left for Australia, then I lived for some time in South Africa. Later I made my way to Europe. I have lived in Switzerland, Austria, and Rome. Finally I decided to take up residence in the Soviet Union. I am now a citizen of this great country. Nevertheless, I still love the American people and I cannot become reconciled to the brainwashing which they are subjected to and which may eventually end in disaster for the land of my birth.

I hope my autobiography will open the eyes of my readers to the great danger threatening the peace – the activities of the United States Central Intelligence Agency abroad.

* * *

I was 28 when I took up my duties as communications technician and code clerk in the American Embassy in New Delhi. My diplomatic rank was that of Assistant Attache.

The American Embassy in India at that time consisted of five sections: executive (ambassador's staff), political, economic, consular, and administrative. The embassy staff also included military, air and naval attaches. The political section was considered the most important. Its official task was to study the political climate of India, the activities of political parties and groups. It contacted government officials and public figures, exerted its influence so as to predispose them to the United States, surveyed the papers, and arranged for the publication of articles, "that would give the local circles and populations a better understanding of the ideals and goals of the United States."

At the same time the political section serves as the main cover of the staff of the intelligence agency.

My wife, Mary London Smith, was on the staff of CIA in the United States. Her work concerned political and labour problems. She had access to the agents' dossiers and was held in high regard because of her ability to cope with practical issues, enlist agents and keep her contacts secret. I don't know whether she was instrumental in the CIA's invitation for me to work for them soon after my arrival in India. Since then I successfully carried out their assignments. My first one was "Operation Lighter."

John Waller,[10] an attaché at the American Embassy in New Delhi, acquainted me with

---

[10] John H. Waller (died Nov. 4, 2004 at 81) is listed in the 1991 membership directory of the Association of Former Intelligence Officers (AFIO). According to Waller's obituaries, he was a former high-ranking official in the CIA who wrote books about espionage and history full time after retiring from the CIA as its inspector general in 1980. Unable to join the military during World War II because of an ear disorder, he got a job overseas as a diplomatic courier for the Foreign Service. In 1943, he joined the Office of Strategic Services (OSS), the predecessor to the CIA, in counterespionage. Later, with the CIA, he served in Iran, Sudan, and India. He was deputy chief of the Africa Division at CIA headquarters (1964-68) and chief of the Near East Division (1971-75). Among his professional honors were the Distinguished Intelligence Medal and the National Civil Service Award. He was chairman of the OSS Society and a member of the board and past president of AFIO. He wrote *The Devil's Doctor: Felix Kersten and the Secret Plot to Turn Himmler Against Hitler* (2002); *Gordon of Khartoum: The Saga of a Victorian Hero* (1988); and *Beyond the Khyber Pass: The Road to British Disaster in the First Afghan War* (1990). See also: Miles Copeland's 1989 book, *The Game Player: Confessions of the CIA's Original Political Operative*; David Corn's 1994 book, *Blond Ghost: Ted Shackley and the CIA's Crusades,* and Hayden Peake's 1992 book, *The Reader's*

"Operation Lighter." Waller was six feet tall and exceedingly strong. He had a long impassive face. It was very misleading – that mask concealed a human dynamo. He carried out his diplomatic duties quickly and nonchalantly. He spent most of his time carrying out espionage for the United States. Waller was on the officer's staff of the CIA. Naturally when he phoned and asked me to come to his office, I began to wonder whether Waller, the diplomat, or Waller, the spy, had called. I met Kaufman,[11] the resident CIA agent in India, in Waller's office.

Breaking Code

With a gesture, Kaufman asked me to sit down and said: "We need your help, Smith. Our relations with," and Kaufman named one of the countries of the third world, "are worse than they have ever been. That country is coming under the influence of the Soviet bloc. We will do everything possible to extend our intelligence operations there. We have the opportunity now to break its code and with your experience, you're the man to do it."

Kaufman knew that during the war, I had been with the group that worked on breaking the Japanese code.

One of our men knows the code clerk of that country's embassy very well, continued Kaufman. His name is Moiz.[12] Our man discovered that Moiz's coding machine has broken down and no one seems to be able to repair it. Perhaps you could. Coding machines aren't classified. Our guy talked Moiz into having them apply to us for help in repairing the machine. He described you as a great specialist in all types of coding machines.

The operation was considered "top secret" of the "top, top, secret"! There is only one room in Washington in which discussion concerning the stealing or buying of foreign codes is permitted. It is under strict armed and electronic guard. However, even the greatest precautionary measures are at times of no avail. For instance, I knew exactly at that time that we were deciphering the codes of the Ministries of Foreign Affairs of Japan and Morocco.

The following morning, besides Waller and Kaufman, John Marsh[13] was present. He was one of the CIA executives in India. His position as Second Secretary of the Embassy was a front for his real activities.

"Permission for going ahead with the Operation has been received," said Kaufman.

Waller spoke up. Turning to me, he said:

"Smith, I'd like to give you some advice. First of all, keep in mind that while you are in the embassy building you will be constantly watched from a secret observation point. Secondly, don't make any movements that might indicate that you are busy with anything else except repairing the machine. Thirdly, observe the layout of the rooms in the embassy, how the

---

Guide to Intelligence Periodicals.

[11] **Smith does not identify Kaufman's full name.**

[12] **Smith does not identify Moiz's full name.**

[13] John Marsh left India in 1958 and was transferred to the Near East as the resident CIA agent in Amman, Jordan. [Note to reader: this was an original footnote (#1) in Smith's book]. **John E. Marsh is listed in the 1968 East German propaganda book,** *Who's Who in CIA***, written by the East German journalist Julius Mader (Thomas Bergner). According to the 1973 US State Department Biographic Register: born 1921, earned a BA from Bates College (1943), served as a captain in the US Army (1943-45), worked as a political officer in the Department of the Army (1950-55), US State Department in New Delhi, India, as a political officer (1955-59), Amman, Jordan (1959-63), political-economic officer in Sri Lanka (1969-71), and a political officer in Kuwait (1971-73).**

building is guarded, and how the work schedule is arranged."

I nodded in assent.

Preparations for "Operation Lighter" went ahead at full speed. "Urgent" cablegrams with questions and instructions kept coming in from the Central Intelligence Agency. Processing of correspondence pertaining to my visit was given priority.

Ronson Lighter

To make things easier, Kaufman gave me a miniature camera concealed in a "Ronson" lighter.[14] It resembled all standard types. However, a close observation revealed that one of its sides was not all made of metal. A small square lens was embedded in the chromium plated surface. This tiny camera could take nineteen pictures without being reloaded. All one had to do was press a tiny button, being careful not to obstruct the view of the lens with one's fingers. The miniature shutter opened simultaneously with the appearance of the flame. A strong spring reloaded the camera and it was ready for the next picture.

Another interesting item was a small case for apparatuses and instruments. Thousands of such small, brown suitcases are made in the United States. But in this case, on the side with the lock, one could write with a screwdriver, match, or even one's fingernail without leaving any traces. Everything that had been written would later become visible.

I had rehearsed all of my "tricks" with the lighter for Marsh, Waller and Kaufman, and repeated the main purpose of the assignment so often that I was fed up.

I had been ordered to thoroughly photograph the embassy's coderoom and find a place for bugging equipment.

It was important to obtain the model and serial number of the coding machine, and photograph the keyboard. I was also to get a sample of the paper ribbon on which the coded text is typed and type in code the letter "A" or any other letter two or three hundred times.

All the walls had to be photographed, especially the wiring and furnishings. I had to remember the worn places on the upholstery, or any part of the walls that were in need of repairs. All papers and documents on the desk had to be photographed. Of course, it was of primary importance that I accomplish all of this while maintaining a calm, natural outward appearance.

At the same time Waller and his wife drove to their hotel which was one-fourth of a mile away. He was having his tea and reading the papers on the hotel verandah. If things went wrong I could get in touch with him quickly. If I got caught, the mighty Waller was to come to my rescue before the embassy staff and the Indian police questioned me and confiscated the tools of my trade.

I was introduced to the embassy staff and offered some excellent coffee. As soon as I entered the code room I photographed everything that was lying on Moiz's desk, while lighting my cigarette. Then, the broken coding machine was brought out and placed on the low coffee table standing in front of the divan. Moiz carefully changed the code setting of the cylinder. This upset me.

I immediately detected the breakdown: a large spring on the main roller had been broken. I didn't have any spare parts with me. I went over the machine with a concentrated air – at the same time photographing the room.

An hour went by. I kept fooling with the machine. Then Moiz brought out an identical

---

[14] **The Ronson lighter company produced a variety of high quality cigar and cigarette lighters. Compared to conventional, boxy Zippo lighters, Ronsons were elegant and fashionable.**

machine and placed it on his desk at some distance from me. He began to set up the key setting to the code on the cylindric mechanism which determined the basis of the cipher system. Then he slowly began to decipher a telegram, striking the keys with two fingers. I pressed the lighter so often that there was a bright flare in the room.

When I was in the midst of my work, Moiz stopped deciphering and glanced at me.

"You smoke a great deal," he said.

My heart was in my mouth. But I managed to blurt out: "Yes, I do," I said.

Moiz went back to his work, his fingers flying over the keyboard. The coded telegrams were in French.[15]

Dizzy with Success

I was dizzy with success. After he had finished deciphering and begun to put the cipher notebook in the safe, I told him I wasn't too familiar with the Swedish coding machines and it would help me a great deal if I could see the one that was in operation. By comparing the two machines I would be able to determine what was wrong with the machine I had been going over for such a long time.

Moiz hesitated for a second, then placed the machine on my table next to the one I was supposed to repair.

I quickly began to strike the letter "A," pretending that I was checking the working of the mechanism. At the same time I lit my cigarette with the lighter and photographed the cylinder with the cipher setting. After coding the letter "A" three hundred times, I quickly hid the ribbon in my pocket. The ribbon plus the photographs of the key to the cipher system, and coding mechanism of the machine, would guarantee that all the coded telegrams sent out by the embassy that day would be decoded by us and in that way we would learn the basic principle of their ciphering system. Actually we had enough information to break their code.

There was nothing more for me to do. I told them that I couldn't repair the machine and pointed out the broken spring. I promised to replace it if they obtained a new one.

I hurried back to the embassy and turned in all my loot to Kaufman and began to write up a report of all the details which were not evident from the photographs.

Waller and his wife were still sitting on the hotel verandah drinking tea. He was still waiting to come to my rescue.

My report was short since all the important information was evident on the photographs. The tiny film from my "lighter" was developed by William Boner.[16] He handled all types of CIA documents since he was in charge of their photo-laboratory, "dark room No. 2." Boner was stationed in Karachi before his transfer to Delhi. He had married in Karachi, was promoted and came on to India. We played golf together. He played a good game, in fact, he was the best golfer in the embassy.

* * *

---

[15] This hints that it could be the Moroccan Embassy in New Delhi. Morocco had been a French protectorate and continued to use the French language in much of its official duties.

[16] William C. Boner Jr. (1927-2011). Buried at Quantico National Cemetery, served in World War II, and is listed in the 1991 and 1996 membership directories of the Association of Former Intelligence Officers. Boner is listed in Mader's 1968 *Who's Who in CIA*, and the 1973 US State Department Biographic Register. Served in Pakistan (1954-57), India (1958-60), Egypt (1961-64), Bolivia (1968-70), and Nicaragua (1970-73).

Three days later Kaufman called on me and informed me that the Central Intelligence Agency thanked and congratulated me on a job well done. I could expect a raise in my salary. My salary was raised after a few weeks and a while later I was even given diplomatic status.

CIA Spies in Indian Secrets

After having carried out my first assignment successfully, I became an active participant in many other operations. I was initiated into the holy of holies of espionage – the organization of contacts with CIA agents in India.

My neighbor, Peter Peterson,[17] a CIA agent, was a specialist in this field. He was also in charge of the installation and upkeep of various "bugging" apparatuses. His intelligence chief was Marelius.[18] The latter was responsible for planning operations and instructing the agents. Peterson and I lived in the same building. We worked together on secret operations in the suburbs of New Delhi. This brought us closer together and eventually we became quite friendly.

One of our objectives was the experimental base of the Indian Air Force on Gurgaon Road.[19] One of our agents worked there. We used to go there once or twice a week for material, as a rule in Peterson's car – a green Ford with a diplomatic license plate. We spent about an hour weaving in and out of the traffic in order to put off anyone that might be tailing us. These trips usually ended without a hitch. The Indians never suspected anything. There was one incident that I've never forgotten. Peterson and I had to sweat plenty through that one.

We started out toward evening weaving our way out to the military air force base. There was no sign of anyone in the rear view mirror. We came to a barbed wire fence four miles from Gurgaon and signs – "Military Zone," and "No Trespassing." We stopped about three hundred meters from the fence. There were fields on both sides of the road. Peterson got out of the car, looked around, and stealthily made his way to the fence. Pete found the hole in the fence that had been made by someone beforehand. And by lying down flat on his stomach was able to crawl under the fence. Of course, it would have been better if we could have obtained our material some other way. But our agent couldn't leave the base.

I remained alone and twilight began to fall. Everything seemed to be hostile – the empty fields, the bushes beyond the barbed wire, and the darkening skies. I was feeling a bit jumpy. If the Indian guard asked me what I was doing here, how as I going to explain my presence? That I had come out for some fresh air? And if they nabbed Pete? Disturbed by these thoughts I kept looking about and was prepared to sound our pre-arranged signal on the horn if danger threatened. Suddenly Pete came on the run as though some dogs were set on him. In a moment he was through the barbed wire rushed to the car and hurled himself into the driver's seat.

---

[17] **Peter Richard Peterson. Listed in the 1969 US State Department Register: born 1931, US Navy (1949-53), US State Department (06/1958) as an S-6 Tech, served in New Delhi, India (1958-61), Vienna, Austria (1961-67), Budapest, Hungary (1961-63), Warsaw, Poland (1965-67), and Tokyo, Japan (1967-69). Also listed in Mader's 1968 propaganda classic,** *Who's Who in CIA*.

[18] Edward Marelius arrived in India in 1958 as First Secretary of the US Embassy (Political Section). This corpulent personage was an important cog in the CIA. In New Delhi he was considered the "brain trust" in the organization of secret meetings. **[Note to reader: this was an original footnote (#2) in Smith's book].** Edward A. Marelius is listed Mader's 1968 *Who's Who in CIA* as serving in India (1958) and Sweden (1968-68).

[19] Air Force Station Gurgaon, Haryana, India.

"What happened?" I asked.

He didn't reply and we were soon travelling at a terrific speed. We were on our way back to town. I remember that crazy ride very well. Although it was dark we didn't turn on our lights. The dim silhouette of the houses and trees raced by. Peterson was silent as though he had been struck speechless.

The car swerved suddenly. There was a loud noise and an outcry. Looking back I saw that we had hit a cyclist.

"Well, he won't be able to remember our number," exclaimed Pete dryly.

When we arrived home we examined the car carefully. There were no signs of any damage – only traces from the bicycle. Peterson wiped them off, then lit a cigarette. I felt exhausted.

"It seems that we've been shadowed," he said at last. Pete pulled out a sharp-edged metal container. "It was always left in the ground under the root of a tree. There would be a rock lying on top of it. Today the container was in its usual place but the rock was missing. I didn't waste any time thinking, just grabbed it and ran. It's quite possible that our agent at the base has been discovered and they are keeping an eye on the hiding place."

Peterson unscrewed the lid of the container pulling out a paper and film.

"Everything seems to be OK, John," he said brightening up. "Now everything depends on the cyclist, if he's alive and noticed our number, then we've had it."

We spent several nerve-racking days but nothing happened. Two weeks later Pete told me that his agent had been in a hurry that day and had been unable to do things properly.

Pete and I worked together without a hitch. There was no attempt to follow us. Americans in India have complete freedom of movement and are trusted by the Indians. That is why we were so surprised when Barbara Peterson, Pete's wife, came bursting into out apartment one day. "John, there's something wrong with our phone. I have a feeling that our phone is tapped. Peter's in Kabul. For God's sake, please check it."

I could hear clicking on the wire and voices speaking in Hindi. Then there was a conversation in English about unloading aviation fuel, the supplying of spare plane-parts and about the training of flyers.

It seems that Peter had been listening in to the conversations of Indian military with the aid of an agent employed by the telephone company. I reassured Barbara that everything was alright.

When Peterson returned to Delhi, I told him about the incident. "The next time you hear something similar, just turn on my tape recorder," he said tersely.

I not only helped Peterson with his espionage – I often accompanied Mary when she contacted her agents. That's how I discovered that the CIA had its own people among the officers of the Indian Army. Incidentally, the CIA often uses women, not only women employees but the wives of their agents. When Mary was pregnant she was much more active in that kind of work. Every evening we met our contacts either in the streets or at restaurants. Because Mary's condition we were never suspected by Indian counter-intelligence, at least that is what the CIA bosses thought. "Mick" was one of the first agents from the Indian Army Headquarters that I had met. I had brought Mary to this rendezvous and remained in the car to observe the situation. We had agreed that if danger threatened, I would get out of the car, raise the hood and get busy with "repairs." Mary was supposed to keep her eye on the car. I saw "Mick" meet her on the corner. They stood in front of a showcase just opposite me. The dimly lit street appeared murky and was practically deserted. Just a few cyclists went by. A ragged little beggar came around the corner.

He came up to me and I gave him a rupee. He was amazed by my generosity and quickly disappeared. I noticed Mary approaching the car.

"You don't look very gay," she said.

"I've been dispensing 'American Aid to India' – I gave a rupee to an urchin[20] and now I'm annoyed with myself. He'll probably return with a whole army of beggars and we'll never get out of here."

Mary grinned ironically.

"I just handed over eight thousand rupees without any regrets!"

"What did you receive in return?" "Documents from the Indian Army Headquarters," replied Mary grasping her bag closely.

"'Mick' did a good job. Jack's pleased with him."

She was referring to Jack Curran,[21] her boss. He was considered one of the most experienced intelligence agents of the CIA in India. He had been here over seven years and knew the country very well. Curran was born in China, grew up in Burma[22] and was educated in the States. He had been approached by the CIA when he was still a student, and they gave him a special grant. The CIA sent him to India to "study sociology." After graduating, Jack was sent to Delhi with the Diplomatic Service. He was with the Embassy's political group for six years but did not hold any important posts. However, he was highly regarded by high ranking members of the diplomatic staff. It was said that Curran was personally acquainted with Allen Dulles.[23] The latter considered him the most valuable man that the USA intelligence ever had in India. He had numerous ties with the country's newspapermen, government employees and high ranking military personnel.

Curran's CIA agents from among the high ranking officers of the Indian Army went by various nicknames: "Mick," "Bill," "Sikh."

The identity to these high ranking members of the Defence Ministry was hidden by other nicknames.

My wife divulged many secrets about CIA agents in top positions in the Indian Army.

One of Mary's close friends was Mrs. Pat Shook, a very attractive woman. She was on the CIA staff and had extensive contacts in India, especially among the military. At one of our evening get-togethers, Pat introduced us to an American journalist, Hamphrey Evans.[24] My wife said:

"Evans has a brilliant future ahead of him. He's one of our agents and carries out important assignments. You have probably heard of General Timmaya's autobiography. He's Chief of Staff of the Indian Armed Forces. Well, Evans wrote his autobiography. The general only signed it. The CIA paid him a tidy sum. However, he didn't achieve fame as a writer – Nehru[25]

---

[20] Street child who is a beggar.

[21] Curran served in India in 1955, according to a 1986 article in the *National Reporter* (formerly known as the anti-CIA periodical *CounterSpy*).

[22] Myanmar.

[23] Allen Dulles (1893-1969) served as CIA deputy director (1951-53) and then director (1953-61). Dulles was a career CIA officer who began his intelligence career during World War II in the Office of Strategic Services (OSS).

[24] Smith misspelled the first name. Humphrey Evans was a freelance journalist. The statement is alleging that the *then* Chief of Army Staff (1957-61) General Kodendera Subayya Thimayya (1906-65) was working for the CIA. Evans wrote numerous books: *Thimayya of India: A Soldier's Life* (1960); *The Adventures of Li Chi a Modern Chinese Legend: In Which a Humble Member of the Working Class Overcomes the Party Establishment* (1967); *The Thought Revolution – University Life and Education in Red China* (1967); and *Escape from Red China* (1964).

[25] Jawaharlal Nehru served as Prime Minister of India (1947-64) and was India's first prime minister after

prevented the book from being published.

"Timmaya is our man, thanks to Evans," continued Mary.

I was amazed at the CIA's ability to penetrate into India's military set-up so thoroughly. Among them was one colonel who held an important position on the General Staff. He was responsible for assigning Indian Military attaches to foreign countries. We were very friendly with him. He often had Sunday dinner with us and we were often his guests.

He was a very influential officer in the Indian military hierarchy. The promotion of the Army officers depended to a great extent on him. So its not surprising that he was sought after by members of the armed forces who were anxious to be in his good graces. In this way he could easily carry out the "assignments" which the CIA had requested in recommending recruits for American Intelligence. His wife was employed by the Canadian High Commission[26] and had every opportunity of making contacts with western diplomats – to be more precise with those whose diplomatic rank was merely a cover for their real activities.

During the relatively long period of our acquaintance with him I observed the change in his standard of living. When we first met, the family was experiencing financial difficulties. When they entertained at that time, they served the most inexpensive liquor available in New Delhi.

Soon it became quite evident that their financial status had brightened. They installed air-conditioning in their bedroom and bought a car. And expensive Scotch whisky was served at their parties. Of course, no one was tactless enough to inquire what had brought about the sudden financial boom but we knew that our Intelligence was at the bottom of it.

He was very generous in giving Mary information about the Indian General Staff Headquarters. He disclosed that there was a group in the Army that was loyal to Nehru and that with Timmaya's blessing he was doing everything possible to prevent the promotion of those officers. His superior officer, General B…[27] of the Personnel Department of the Indian Army's Headquarters, was often our guest.

The General was an interesting individual. He had been India's Military Attache in Washington for several years. He had been influenced by the "American way of life" to such an extent that he was more American than Nixon! The General was friendly with the American Military Attache, Curtis.[28]

He frequently gave my wife information. Once during our vacation when Mary and I went to Simla,[29] Bannerjee[30] arrived there unexpectedly. Skipping the formalities he said he had important business to talk over. He knew that I knew what the score was and didn't hesitate to speak in my presence. He handed over a list of names of officers who according to him were trying to oppose the army clique in power.

In carrying out their activities, American intelligence relied mainly on a group of high ranking Indian officers who opposed the Prime Minister's policies and who were pro-American. Although the Indian Army was of primary interest for the Americans, it was also a bone of

---

independence from Britain.

[26] **Canada's Embassy.**

[27] **It is unclear who Smith is referring to here or why his full name, assuming it was Bannerjee, was left out.**

[28] **Smith often mentions individuals without full names. I was unable to identify "Curtis."**

[29] **The capital city of the Indian state of Himachal Pradesh, located in northern India.**

[30] **It is unclear from my research who "General Bannerjee" is exactly. He is only mentioned twice in Smith's book with no reference to his full name or service.**

contention between them and the British. Britain, traditionally, had always greatly influenced the Indian Armed Forces. Now she had to contend with her rival, the Americans. On several occasions when the Americans wanted to sell arms to India they crossed swords with the British military attaches.

American military attaches always tried to corner the market for disposing of arms in the countries of the British Commonwealth.

The CIA and US Military Intelligence gained entry to the high ranking military circles of India, and tried to influence them. They did not begrudge funds, time, or personnel for this purpose.

Washington constantly stressed the need for a pro-American group in the Indian Army that could take over at the opportune moment. With this goal in mind, the American Intelligence did not confine its activities to the Indian capital. They set up a network that covered the entire country and planted their agents in both the lower and higher echelons of the military. I recall a secret document that arrived from Washington indicating that all military personnel that had close ties with us should be promoted to more influential positions and place an officer at the head of the Indian General Staff who could direct an Indian policy that would be advantageous to us.

According to the document, agents in the American Consulates in the various cities of India were to concentrate on the higher ranking officers of the garrisons and find out their political outlook, their attitude to the USA. Ultimately the best candidates would be recruited for the CIA. The methods used were neither above-board nor subtle. "Ralph" was the nickname of an Indian colonel whom the CIA got in their clutches. They were aware that he had a weakness for the fair sex. So they went "fishing" for him using an American beauty, a CIA agent of course, as bait. The colonel snapped at the bait and was caught, hook, line and sinker. So the CIA added another name to their list of American agents in India.

The American Intelligence Agency was constantly broadening its ties with the army and also the political circles of India. Every attempt was made to influence outstanding political figures who could in turn influence government policy or at least, were well informed concerning it.

One of those who became a CIA agent was known as "Plutarch."[31] That, of course, is not his real name and I do not want to divulge it. I knew him very well. I found his association with the American Intelligence very trying, and he did not willingly become an agent. The CIA gradually laid a very clever trap for him. And once you're caught, it isn't easy to escape. Furthermore, "Plutarch" had a very gentle disposition and could not cope with the situation.

"Plutarch" held a responsible position and had access to classified material of the Indian Government. He knew all about the government's current problems.

"Plutarch" used to visit us. As a rule, he came late in the evening when it was dark and instead of using the parking lot he would park his car in the darkest corner of the courtyard.

A deep friendship developed and Jack Curran took advantage of it. He called me in and said: "From what your wife tells me, your contacts with 'Plutarch' have been successful. He's afraid of getting burned and that's why he is so careful. We need some one whom he trusts. So far your wife had contact with him but she is not always able to meet him. We can't afford to procrastinate with him. When your wife can't contact him, you will take over. All information, documents in particular, will be turned over to me immediately. Then you personally will return them to him."

---

[31] Whether this is Smith's attempt at hinting to the real identity of the person is unclear. Historically, Plutarch was an ancient philosopher and writer who lived in Rome (AD 45-120).

"Think it over and organize it in such a manner that no one will suspect anything." As a rule, when I had to contact "Plutarch" instead of Mary, we met during the day. "Plutarch" would phone and say, it was "Raj" speaking and ask me to come and see him. We had six pre-arranged meeting places, one for each day of the week.

I usually arrived first in order to check whether he was being "tailed." There was never any sign to this effect. Evidently "Plutarch" was not under suspicion.

We received documents from "Plutarch" indicating the changes that were being contemplated in the Indian Government, including the Ministry of Foreign Affairs. As a result, the CIA knew what steps were being planned by the Indian Government, whom the Prime Minister was meeting or planning to meet and his opinions on various matters. "Plutarch" was adequately reimbursed for his information. I personally turned over a total of 34,000 rupees to him during several visits.

The CIA exerted great influence on India's economy and politics through one of Indian ministers. India has a great potential market for US agricultural products. The market was threatened when the Indian Government decided to develop the national production of grain and other products. The best way to achieve this was the organization of cooperatives made up of the numerous unproductive small farm holdings. The Cooperative farm societies become part of the Congress Party's and government's program.

The CIA personnel in India were given the task of discrediting the program in order to retain India as a market for American agricultural products.

To achieve the goal the CIA used one of the Indian ministers.

His consultants were representatives of the Cooperative Union of the USA,[32] Thomas Keen and Alex Felder. For a large sum of money the agreed to influence the leaders to speak up against the Cooperative farm societies and sabotage the government's program. What a paradox – the cooperative union against cooperatives. One of the uninitiated in the US Embassy said jokingly that soon the heads of the union would be unemployed if the cooperative deal fell through! David Burgess[33] then replied smilingly: "We paid them enough to keep them from worrying about the future!"

American intelligence had an agent whom I heard referred to as "Pike" close to circles connected with the Indian Prime Minister's chancellery. Relying on "Pike's" information, the American Intelligence planned and carried out a campaign that would discredit the "leftist" personnel and place the people they needed nearer to the top government posts.

According to one of the CIA agents, in the embassy, "Pike" gave the agency information

---

[32] National Farmers Union (Farmers' Educational and Cooperative Union of America) is a national federation of state Farmers Union organizations in the US).

[33] Served in India (1956) and Indonesia (1967). See: David Burgess' 2000 memoir: *Fighting for Social Justice: The Life Story of David Burgess*. According to Amazon books: "David Burgess's commitment to social justice began in his youth and continued throughout his studies at Oberlin College. After college he helped coal miners to build homes and organized sharecroppers and migrant workers as part of the Southern Tenant Farmers Union. He was an active member of the Congress of Industrial Organizations (CIO) and headed up the CIO State Council in Georgia. He fought to improve the conditions of industrial and agricultural workers in India, served in the Foreign Service in India, with the Peace Corps in Indonesia, and in East Asia with UNICEF [United Nations Children's Fund], and later fought for affirmative action and public housing as a Christian minister in Newark, New Jersey. *Fighting for Social Justice* is the memoir of a man committed to achieving social justice for the poor. Through his narrative, David Burgess connects his fight for the welfare of others to broader politics of twentieth-century America. Burgess combines his belief in pacifism, work with international aid agencies, and inner city Christian ministry to demonstrate the connections between international social movements in America, Canada, and Asia."

about Mathai,[34] the chief secretary of the Prime Minister's chancellery. "Pike" described him as being extremely obnoxious and rabidly anti-American. "Pike" wrote that Mathai was concerned with the government economic policy which could be used to accuse him of graft.

On the basis of "Pike's" information, and with the help of Curran, a program of action to undermine Mathai was worked out. I don't know whether Mathai really had dealings with private business or not, nevertheless the American intelligence by making use of "Pike's" information made a mountain out of a molehill. With the help of the CIA in India, Mathai was accused of receiving large bribes from Indian businessmen for supposedly favoring them in government contracts. Mathai was forced to resign.

In their campaign against India the United States was aided by CIA agents on the staff of other countries' missions in India. They included diplomats, correspondents, businessmen, tourists and many others. This category of agents was carefully concealed from the British and other American allies. In other words, the CIA used the intelligence services of its allies in organizing an all-out system of espionage.

One of the most outstanding agents in this category was the Philippine Ambassador to India, Manuel Alzate.[35] He arrived in India in January 1959 and soon had the reputation of being a Don Juan.[36] Alzate concentrated on the wives and relatives of government employees and the military. In a short period of time he made friends in the Ministry of Foreign Affairs and among the army officers. He turned over his information to Charles Cogan,[37] an American Attache in the political department, with whom he was friendly. Another close friend of the Philippine Ambassador was John Lund, vice-director of the United States Information Service[38] in New Delhi, and on the staff of the CIA. Alzate gave vital information about the foreign policy of the Indian Government and leading Army personnel, the disposition of Indian troops in

---

[34] M.O. Mathai (1909-81) was assistant to India's first Prime Minister, Jawaharlal Nehru. Mathai worked with the US Army in India before becoming an assistant to Nehru in 1946. He resigned in 1959 following Communist allegations of misuse of power and spying. Despite the allegations, Nehru remained close. He published his controversial memoirs in *Reminiscences of the Nehru Age* (1978) and *My Days with Nehru* (1979).

[35] Manuel A Alzate (1896-1964) served as an assemblyman for the Nueva Ecijia Province, 1st District, during the 1935-1938 First Assembly of the Philippines, ambassador to Australia (1948), Consul General to the Philippine Consulate in Honolulu (1949-52), Ambassador to Pakistan (1957-58) and India (October 1958).

[36] Don Juan is a fictional character who devotes his life to seducing women and going on adventures. He first appears in European literature in 1630.

[37] Charles G. Cogan (born 1928) is an academic and former CIA agent (1954-91). At the CIA, Cogan's roles included chief of the Near East and South Asia Division in the CIA's Directorate of Operations (1979-84) and Paris station chief (1984-89). According to the 1973 US State Department Biographic Register: Charles G. Cogan, born 1928, graduated Harvard University (1949), served in the US Army (1951-53) as a second lieutenant (1954-57), served as a foreign affairs officer in the US Department of Defense, US State Department as a political officer (1957), Leopoldville (1963), Khartoum (1965), and Rabat (1971). According to Bob Woodward's 2005 book, *Veil: The Secret Wars of the CIA, 1981-1987*, Cogan's CIA service included serving as an operations officer in India, Congo, Sudan, and Morocco. "He had a chilly, all-business handshake, and eyes like a detective. A modest, barely noticeable scar down one side of his face heightened the effect." See also Chapter 17, "Cogan's Last Stand," in George Crile's 2003 book, *Charlie Wilson's War*, and Steve Coll's 2004 book, *Ghost Wars: The Secret History of the CIA, Afghanistan, and bin Laden, from the Soviet Invasion to September 10, 2001*.

[38] Known later as the United States Information Agency (USIA). It was disbanded in 1999, with some operations, such as the Voice of America and Radio Free Europe, placed under the Broadcasting Board of Governors.

Kashmir[39] and Rajasthan.[40]

The US Central Intelligence Agency resorted to all means in stirring up enmity between the people of Pakistan and India. The Naga tribesmen[41] who began a separatist movement and wanted to establish an independent state of Nagaland, received extensive aid from the Americans. In the fall of 1956, a CIA agent with the Technical Cooperation Mission, made a trip to Imphal[42] with the aid of the American Military Attache. A secret meeting with the leaders of the Naga tribesmen was held there.

The American Intelligence handed over several million rupees and arms to the leaders of the tribesmen. At that same meeting they were given secret instructions that had been prepared in Washington. Accordingly, they were to come out in active opposition to the Indian Army and use arms if necessary. Their goal was to break away from the Indian Council of States. It was planned that the separatists would try to hold out until the Americans came to their aid.

The US Consul General and CIA agent in Dacca held a secret meeting with the leaders of the Naga movement. It was held in Eastern Pakistan just across the border from India. He gave the separatists large sums of money and instructions. Washington insisted on openly extending the political movement for the break-away from India. Joseph Macaller,[43] a CIA agent, was in charge of delivering arms from Eastern Pakistan to the Nagaland tribesmen. He was aided by John Grover[44] and American diplomats in Dacca.[45] The group's contact in Delhi was with Clara Pappas.

David Henry Blee[46] was among those who organized the delivery of arms and ammunition to the Naga rebels, and the training of guerilla in Eastern Pakistan.[47] He began his career in Pakistan in 1950 as an attaché in the American Embassy. He co-ordinated his activities with the

---

[39] A territory under Indian administration in northern India and is in dispute with Pakistan over control.

[40] India's largest territory by size, borders Pakistan in the northeast.

[41] Nagaland is a state in northeast India bordering Assam to the west, Arunachal Pradesh and part of Assam to the north, Myanmar to the east and Manipur to the south. With 16 different tribes, the state has experienced insurgency as well as inter-ethnic conflict since the 1950s.

[42] The city of Imphal is the capital of the Indian state of Manipur, in the same general area of Nagaland.

[43] Joseph Macaller is mentioned in the 1984 anti-CIA book by Pauly V. Parakal, *Secret Wars of CIA*. Nothing more appears on the Internet or other resources. It is possible that Smith misspelled his name, but different spellings did not reveal anything.

[44] John Grover is mentioned in the 1984 anti-CIA book by Pauly V. Parakal, *Secret Wars of CIA*.

[45] Dhaka, Bangladesh.

[46] Blee (1916-2000) was a decorated CIA agent. See obituary in the *Guardian* (August 22, 2000) by Harold Jackson, "CIA Chief Who Rescued the Agency from Paranoia." According to a variety of sources: Blee served in Pakistan (1949-54), South Africa (1954-57), and India (1962-68). Blee is listed in the 1990 membership directory of the Veterans of OSS. He is mentioned in the following books: Milt Bearden's 2004 book, *The Main Enemy: The Inside Story of the CIA's Final Showdown with the KGB*; Edward Jay Epstein's 1989 book, *Deception: The Invisible War Between the KGB and the CIA*; Julius Mader's 1968 propaganda book, *Who's Who in CIA*; Tom Mangold's 1991 book, *Cold Warrior: James Jesus Angleton, the CIA's Master Spy Hunter*; Ted Morgan's 1999 book, *A Covert Life: Jay Lovestone - Communist, Anti-Communist, and Spymaster*; 1969 U.S. State Department Biographic Register; David Wise's 1992 book, *Molehunt: The Secret Search for Traitors that Shattered the CIA*; and David Wise's 1988 book, *The Spy Who Got Away*.

[47] Present day Bangladesh, which was separated from Pakistan after the 1971 Bangladesh Liberation War.

CIA agents in India. I learned later that after he had organized spy network in the US Consulate in Dacca, Blee left for Delhi in 1962.

In 1956, David Burgess, a recent arrival in India, joined in the activities of extending the separatist movement in the border districts of Pakistan. This tall, lean individual, gave one the impression that he was weighed down with care. He was the father of a family of six. Burgess was fond of speaking about God and would often read the Bible at church services in the Embassy.

This open exterior concealed another Burgess – that of a CIA agent. His post as an embassy attaché served as a cover for his CIA activities. He made frequent trips to the districts of the separatists tribesmen and had secret meetings with their leaders. A. Chapman, a young officer, was one of his aides. Some Pakistani diplomats, especially the military attaché, maintained close ties at that time with the CIA in the American Embassy. He had contacted his colleagues in the US Embassy in New Delhi on several occasions. The CIA gave him information concerning the preparation of the Indian government's policy, its relations with Nagaland, the arming and disposition of Indian armed forces, and the plans of the Indian General Staff Headquarters.

* * *

The United States Central Intelligence Agency did not hesitate to use blackmail, slander, misinformation, sabotage and murder in carrying out its evil work.

The whole world knows about the tragic disaster that struck the Indian airliner. "The Princess of Kashmir,"[48] in the Spring of 1955. It was on a special run from Peking to Bandung. On board were the participants of the Congress of the Peoples of Asia and Africa devoted to peaceful coexistence and solidarity of the peoples in their struggle against the colonial yoke. The intelligence services of the imperialist countries, the United States, CIA in particular, were bent on finding a way to prevent the Bandung Conference.[49]

That was the primary purpose in sabotaging the "Princess of Kashmir." This has been verified by the finds of an authoritative commission that investigated the causes of the disaster and the testimony of the liner's engineer, Anant Shridar Karnik, who remained alive. The documentary evidence was both dramatic and tragic.

"The Princess of Kashmir" was on its way to Djakarta.[50] It had taken off from the Hongkong Airport five and a half hours previously. The airliner was flying at an altitude of six thousand meters.[51] Suddenly a blast in the luggage compartment rent the air. The plane's fuselage was filled with swirls of acrid smoke. The terrified passengers could see the wings of the plane being devoured by flames. The aluminum burned as though it were paper. Large

---

[48] Air India. Flight was carrying eight members of the Chinese delegation, a Vietnamese, and two European journalists.

[49] Known as the Bandung Conference it was first large-scale Asian-African conference and was held in April 1955 in Bandung, Indonesia. Twenty-five countries participated and organized by Indonesia, China, Burma, India, Pakistan, and Ceylon (Sri Lanka). There were suspicions in the CIA that this was an anti-US effort to subvert Western influence in the Third World by the Soviets.

[50] Jakarta, Indonesia.

[51] 19,685 feet.

chunks of molten metal began to break away. It was 160 miles to the nearest airport in Singapore. Enveloped in flames and smoke the airliner began to lose altitude rapidly. The planes fuselage was red hot. Captain Jatar decided to land in the sea. The plane hit the sea with great force. A hot jet of gasoline and oil hissed from the tanks. The sea surrounding the plane was on fire. By some miracle, besides Karnik, the plane's pilot Dikshit and the navigator Pathak were also saved. They swore that they would tell the whole world about the sabotage. At their initiative, the Indonesian Government set up a special investigating commission to ascertain the causes of the disaster. The commission stated that the airliner had been blown up by a delayed action time bomb that had been placed in the left landing gear of the plane. The remains of the bomb were found in the sea and were eloquent proof of sabotage.

Imagine my surprise when I discovered two years later that I had been unwittingly involved in the sabotage of the "Princess of Kashmir." Harry Rozitske,[52] the new CIA chief in India told me about it after "Operation Lighter" had been successfully carried out.

I recalled that in the Spring of 1955, Jack Curran, US Attache in Delhi, and I learned later that he was on the staff of CIA, had asked me to do him a small favour. He called me into his office and said:

"Mr. Smith, something has to be delivered urgently to one of our friends. Could you go the

---

[52] Harry Rozitske arrived in India in 1957. As the CIA chief in the country his activities deserve more attention. I plan to write about him in the future. **[Note to reader: this was an original footnote (#3) in Smith's book].** Smith misspells his name numerous times in the book. Should be "Rositzke." I corresponded with Rositske in April 1993 and his response was as follows: "I don't remember Smith at all. Smith's story is a total fabrication. Moscow could not even spell my name straight, although the KGB officers in Delhi knew me well." According to his 1981 book, *The KGB: The Eyes of Russia* (Doubleday, 1981; page 164), Rositzke makes only one reference to Smith: "In spite of their persistent explorations the KGB had only one success that we know of – and it is not even clear whether the American, a State Department code clerk, was recruited in New Delhi or on a subsequent assignment in Southeast Asia. What we do know is that the code clerk, John Disco Smith, somehow ended up in Moscow as the tool for an anti-American propaganda campaign by the unofficial Peace and Progress radio. The preliminary Moscow broadcasts exposed some of the vile episodes the CIA had supposedly been guilty of in southern Asia, including the imaginary exploits of the CIA station chief in Delhi. The broadcasts also promised a further cloak-and-dagger series in which I was apparently to be the hero, but they never came off. Perhaps the audience reaction to the pilot did not achieve a high enough rating." According to his obituary published in the *New York Times* on November 8, 2002: Harry Rositzke, 91, 1911-2002, served as an intelligence officer for nearly 30 years, first with the Office of Strategic Services and with its successor, the CIA, Rositzke found himself at the center of wartime and then cold war covert activity. He also found himself in an unwanted limelight. Once, an office he led was accused of involvement in a failed attempt on the life of the Chinese leader Zhou Enlai. On another occasion there were suspicions, never substantiated, that he had been picked to lead an illegal CIA domestic spying operation. Rositzke was the first chief of the CIA's Soviet division. From 1952-54, he ran agents against the Soviet Union and Eastern Europe out of Munich. From 1954-56, he was in charge of the operations schools in the agency's training division. In 1957, he moved to New Delhi as station chief, operating against Soviet, Chinese and Tibetan targets. In 1962, Rositzke returned to Washington where he recruited Soviet and Eastern European diplomats as informers there and in New York. But in 1967 a former State Department code clerk, John Discoe Smith, who served in India from 1954 to 1959 and later defected to the Soviet Union, published a pamphlet in which he asserted that Rositzke had been expelled from India at his instigation. Smith said he had written to Indian officials telling them that the CIA's New Delhi station had been involved in the 1955 bombing of a plane carrying the Chinese delegation to the Bandung Nonaligned Conference in the mistaken belief that Zhou Enlai was on board. India then expelled Rositzke in belated retaliation, Smith said. After a period at George Washington's Sino-Soviet Institute, Rositzke was coordinator of operations against Communist parties abroad until his retirement in 1970. Five years later, however, he found himself back in the news when the director of central intelligence, William E. Colby, published a report on the agency's illegal domestic spying operations, known as Chaos. The operations had begun under President Lyndon Johnson but were expanded by President Richard Nixon.

"Maidens' Hotel[53] immediately? They'll be waiting for you."

I smiled.

"The name suits me," I said jokingly. "I wonder what kind of a maiden is waiting for me?"

"Smith, there isn't any girl waiting for you," he replied seriously.

"You are supposed to meet a fellow by the name of Van Fen.[54] Tell him that I sent you and give him this bag. It's rather heavy."

"What's in it?"

"Smith, I can't tell you because I don't know," replied Curran.

"We received it sealed with instructions to deliver it without opening."

"You are strong, John. I'm sure you can manage it," continued Curran. "Get going as fast as you can and handle it as gently as you would a new born babe. There's a very delicate mechanism in the bag. Let me help you carry it to the car."

I drove out of the Embassy and started for Old Delhi. I passed through the massive "Delhi Gate," and soon came to the Daryaganj Market.[55] The streets were congested with cars and all kinds of vehicles – the most unusual means of conveyance. Passing "Chandni Chauk" or "Silver Street," I enjoyed a fleeting glimpse of the red Jain Temple.[56] In a few minutes I stopped in front of an insignificant-looking building, that was the Maidens' Hotel.

The Indian porters rushed to open the door of my car and wanted to help me with my luggage. I hurriedly thrust some coins in their hands and entered the foyer. A young man in a light tusah silk suit shot with a shade of gold, met me in a room on the second floor. He took my bag quickly and placed it carefully on the davenport. Then Van Fen asked me to be seated near a small table and opened of a pack of cigarettes which had been lying on it.

The cigarettes did not look familiar but their taste reminded me of a fine brand of French tobacco.

Van Fen poured me a cup of strong fragrant tea, remarking that such tea was not available anywhere in India. According to my host, Lundtsien tea[57] was the finest in the world. He wasn't very talkative, just sipped his tea and scrutinized me. He said he was leaving Delhi and that a plane was waiting for him. As I took my leave he presented me with a sandalwood fan painted with weeping willows, pavilions with tile-covered roofs turned up at the corners, and Chinese junks.[58]

I returned to the Embassy and told Curran that I had done as he wished. He replied that he knew that and added that Fen had already flown from India.

---

[53] Established in 1903, the hotel today takes a nostalgic pride in its past. Due to its colonial/oriental unique architecture it is often used as a location to make movies.

[54] "Van Fen" is not a normal Chinese name, it appears to actually be "Wang Feng."

[55] Daryaganj Market ("River Trading Post/Warehouse") is a Delhi neighborhood inside the walled city of Shahjahanabad (Old Delhi).

[56] Shri Digambar Jain Lal Mandir is the oldest Jain temple in Delhi.

[57] It is unclear what kind of tea this might be. The Internet produced no references to it, though it appears to be partly Chinese (*tsien* = thousand). It is possible this is a hint to Ven Fen's identity, but this is speculation. It is also possible it is Llantén (Spanish), known as Plantain (in English), which is a rare medicinal plant sometimes made into a tea.

[58] A "junk" is a Chinese boat commonly seen in Hong Kong.

I had practically forgotten about the incident, when Harry Rozitske, after the successful Cipher operation, said to me: "We're indebted to you, John. You were taking a big risk when you delivered that bag to the Maidens' Hotel." Harry gave no further explanation. After Mary and I were married, she told me that there had been two time bombs in the bag.[59]

Neither the diplomats nor CIA agents were willing to take a chance on having to return with the bag or fall into the clutches of the police. Therefore it had been decided to give me the job without telling me what it was all about. Van Fen, who had taken my bag at the Maidens' Hotel, was a member of the Kuomintang.[60] He had fled from China to Hongkong and worked for Curran.

At the time there was a great deal I would like to have said to Mr. Curran, my wife's boss. However, I would have let down Mary – after all she had divulged the information in great secrecy. Then and there I decided I would never forgive my bosses for their trickery.

The CIA's contacts with the Kuomintang grew and expanded. At the end of the summer of 1957, a group of Kuomintangs arrived in Delhi with the US Consul General from Calcutta. A secret meeting between the group and CIA representatives was arranged in the US Embassy. A program for the Calcutta group's activities was worked out. With the group's aid contact was made with the Kuomintangs in Burma.[61] The subsequent incidents on the Indian-Burmese frontier had been prepared and carried out with the direct participation of the US Central Intelligence Agency. James Burns[62] maintained contact with the Kuomintang. He arrived in India in 1957. His position as Third Secretary of the US Embassy was a cover for his CIA activities.

* * *

The United States Information Service in India is just one of the branches of the Central Intelligence Agency. The American spies would be deprived of their communication network if it were not for the USIS. The latter rent teletype facilities from the Indian government which gives the USIS direct communication with Calcutta, Bombay, Madras and the main office in New Delhi. Although the facilities are rented by USIS, they are used primarily by the CIA and the Embassy. The agreement between USIS and the Indian government which specifically indicates that the facilities are to be used by the USIS only, was circumvented. These machinations deprive the Indian government of 250,000 to 300,000 dollars annually.

---

[59] If true, most likely timers and not actual bombs.

[60] The Kuomintang (KMT) (Chinese Nationalist Party) lost the Chinese civil war against the Chinese Communist Party and was forced to flee mainland China and base itself on the island of Taiwan (Formosa). The KMT continues to exist today on Taiwan, but has lost much of its political strength since the end of martial law in 1991. Taiwan is now a thriving democracy.

[61] Now known as Myanmar. At the end of the Chinese civil war elements of the KMT army had been pushed out of China into Burma (Myanmar), as well as Nepal, Russia, and Vietnam. Though the KMT government set up its capital in Taiwan, it kept a tight rein on KMT elements in these countries until they were either eradicated by local forces, transported to Taiwan, or melted into local societies. KMT elements in northern Burma are famous for their involvement in the opium trade. See also: Bertil Lintner's 1999 book, *Burma in Revolt: Opium and Insurgency Since 1948*.

[62] James B. Burns served in Burma (1953), India (1957), and Indonesia (1961-67). See also: 1964 US State Department Foreign Service List, and David Wise's 1995 book, *Nightmover: How Aldrich Ames Sold the CIA to the KGB for $4.6 Million*.

The US Information Service in India has a complete network that covers the whole territory of India. Over three and a half million dollars have been appropriated annually for its operation.

Many people are under the impression that the USIS in India is only an educational and information project. However, its main aim is to act as a supplement and help to the CIA.

The first USIS chief in New Delhi was Timberlake,[63] America's master spy in India. This CIA agent was experienced in espionage. It was indicative when he was sent to India in 1947 to head the USIS that it would be used from its very inception for espionage. He co-ordinated his work closely with George Allen,[64] an outstanding agent and the American Ambassador in India. Incidentally, later Allen became the director of the US Information Agency.

The majority of the USIS personnel in India were either directly or indirectly connected with the CIA and the Federal Bureau of Investigation. Among them were Frank Dorrey, John Flanagan, John Lund and Robert Lee.

The Calcutta branch of the USIS also had close ties with the CIA. Its staff and agents included the head of the branch office of USIS, Glenn Leigh Smith, Thomas Needham, and US Consulate employees in Calcutta, Walter Campbell,[65] and Charles Shannon – all of them CIA agents.

The situation is the same in the other USIS branches – such as Bombay and Madras.

The USIS provided a cover for the gathering of information concerning outstanding government and political leaders in India, their differences, important decisions and projects of the Indian government in foreign and domestic affairs and conflicts between the central and state governments.

For instance, Mr. Dorrey of the Calcutta USIS office, gathered espionage information pertaining to the main direction of Indian policy. The Censor Department of the USIS office was

---

[63] Possibly "Clare Hayes Timberlake" (1907-82) who was the first US Ambassador to the Congo (Zaire) (1960-61) during the violent transition from being a Belgian colony. Joined the Foreign Service in 1930 after attending Harvard graduate school. His first post was at the consulate in Toronto, and later served in Buenos Aires (Argentina 1957-58), Montevideo, Zurich, Vigo, Spain, Aden, Bombay, New Delhi (India 1948-52), Hamburg (Germany 1952-60), Lima (Peru 1955-57), and Bonn. After the Congo, served as special assistant in the US State Department and with the Arms Control and Disarmament Agency. Retired in 1970 as a member of the Board of Examiners of the Foreign Service and the State Department's Bureau of Public Affairs. Spoke Arabic, French, German, Italian, Portuguese and Spanish. See also Dougall Richardson's 1973 book, *U.S. State Department. United States Chiefs of Mission 1778-1973*; David Gibbs' 1991 book, *The Political Economy of Third World Intervention: Mines, Money, and U.S. Policy in the Congo Crisis*; Sean Kelly's 1993 book, *America's Tyrant: The CIA and Mobutu of Zaire*; and the *Who's Who in America* (1962-1963). Note to reader: extensive government archival data on Timberlake is referenced in Ludo De Witte's 2002 book, *The Assassination of Lumumba*.

[64] George Venable Allen (1903-1970). After finishing graduate work at Harvard University in 1929 served as US Ambassador to Iran (1946-48), Assistant Secretary of State for Public Affairs (1948-49), U.S. Ambassador to Yugoslavia (1949-52), US Ambassador to India/Nepal (1952-53), Assistant Secretary of State for Near Eastern, South Asian, and African Affairs (1953-54), U.S. Ambassador to Greece (1956-57), and Director of the USIS from (1957-60). See also James Bill's 1988 book, *The Eagle and the Lion: The Tragedy of American-Iranian Relations*; Wilbur Crane Eveland's 1980 book, *Ropes of Sand: America's Failure in the Middle East*; Fitzhugh Green's 1988 book, *American Propaganda Abroad*; Sallie Pisani's 1991 book, *The CIA and the Marshall Plan*; and Dougall Richardson's 1973 book, *U.S. State Department. United States Chiefs of Mission 1778-1973*.

[65] Walter L. Campbell served in Turkey (1955-57), Syria (1955), and India (1957-69). See also: Wilbur Crane Eveland's 1980 book, *Ropes of Sand: America's Failure in the Middle East*; Mader's 1968 book, *Who's Who in CIA*; and 1969 U.S. State Department Biographic Register.

concerned with espionage information concerning political and economic problems.

Hobart Luppi,[66] a CIA agent, was employed by the FBI for a number of years. He was a graduate of the University of Oklahoma and spent several years in Cairo as a Security Officer. In 1955 he was sent to New Delhi. He spent about two years there and during that time made great strides in studying Hindi. He returned to the United States and continued his studies in Hindi at the University of California. In 1959 he returned to India and worked in the economic sphere. Luppi had extensive ties with the Indian police. They were helpful in covering up several American espionage failures in India.

With the help of the USIS, the CIA, besides gathering information, disseminates distorted information. This is done through the local papers.

Many foreign organizations and papers have ties with the Indian press and those of other countries. All embassies send material concerning their country to editorial offices. There is nothing wrong with this. But things take on a different aspect when representatives of foreign countries under the cover of disseminating information, secretly contact employees of information ministries, editors, radio correspondents, newspapers and journals, who for a price are willing to publish deliberately biased articles, foist ideas on the readers which would be in the interests of the Intelligence Service and US propaganda.

This is how the United States Information Service operates in India. All USIS employees are obliged to do their utmost in having specially selected materials and events about America, India, and other countries published in the Indian press. Certain papers and journals are financed by the USIS and large sums are paid to the publishers and chief editors.[67]

I could name a number of Indian journalists that had been won over by the Americans. An example is Ram Singh, editor of the journal *Thought* who regularly published materials from the USIS under the names of Indians. Nikhil Maitra, director of the "Eastern India News Agency" was the man who wrote the book *Violence in Tibet*.[68] The main chapters were based on CIA material.

Glenn Leigh Smith of the Calcutta Branch of USIS had a diligent aide. He was Amar Ghosh, assistant editor of the *Hindustan Standard*. Ghosh published everything that was in the interests of the United States. Atul Krishna Ghosh, the owner and editor of the monthly *Pradeep*, also published articles ordered by us which were published in his paper under his name. Certain Misra translated books selected by the Americans for India in the Oriya language. He is considered one of the chief CIA agents in the State of Orissa.[69] I knew that some Indian papers that were subsidized by CIA through USIS. They included the *Indian Express*[70] and *Thought*. The

---

[66] Not CIA. Luppi served at the US Embassy in India as second secretary, economic section, in 1959. Luppi later served as the Consul General in Karachi, Pakistan. Luppi is mentioned as a US State Department "Aviation Liaison Division" in *Department of State Foreign Relations Of The United States, 1964–1968*, Volume XXXIV, Energy Diplomacy And Global Issues, Document 122, Memorandum of Conversation (October 8, 1965); *Foreign Relations Of The United States, 1969–1976*, Volume E-7, Documents On South Asia, 1969–1972, Document 200, Telegram 26 From the Consulate General in Karachi to the Department of State, 1154Z (January 3, 1972).

[67] An excellent study on the CIA's Cold War efforts to influence academia and media outlets is Peter Coleman's 1989 book: *The Liberal Conspiracy: The Congress for Cultural Freedom and the Struggle for the Mind of Postwar Europe*. Another good book referencing CIA support for media outlets and academia in Asia was written by retired CIA officer Joseph B. Smith, *Portrait of a Cold Warrior: Second Thoughts of a Top CIA Agent* (1981). Also see: Brian Crozier's 1993 autobiography, *Free Agent: The Unseen War 1941-1991*.

[68] It is not clear if this is a reference to Maitra's book, *Rape of Tibet* (A. Biswas, 1963).

[69] Now called Odisha, located in eastern India.

[70] An English-language newspaper published in Mumbai (Bombay), India.

political observer of the *Indian Express*, Frank Moraes[71] and editor of *Current*, Karaka maintained close ties with the CIA.

Every year the USIS selects a dozen journalists recommended by the CIA and organizes a three-month visit to the United States with all expenses paid. The same number is selected as candidates for the following year. It is quite understandable that they are loyal to the Americans and write whatever they dictate. Occasionally the CIA through the offices of the USIS sends these journalists with the correspondents' group accompanying the country's leaders abroad.

The CIA pays particular attention to those journalists that write critical articles about America's foreign policy and the American way of life. The Information Agency keeps track of such journalists and as soon as their articles appear they immediately take measures to suppress their "undesirable" career as journalists. Sometimes an employee of USIS attempts to influence or buy the journalists. If this doesn't work, he resorts to outright blackmail, using materials and methods of the US Central Intelligence Agency. I recall that in 1959 the paper *People's Guardian* in Chandigarh[72] published a very critical article about American propaganda in the Punjab. The American Embassy was very displeased with the article. An employee of USIS was sent to see the editor at his apartment and without much ado offered him a large sum of money to prevent similar articles from being published. Soon the paper changed its attitude toward the Americans and became subservient to their interests. In some instances pressure is brought to bear on the journalists.

Books by writers and journalists willing to cooperate with the US Intelligence and whose writings reflect the right attitude toward the United States are published. Outlines, factual material, and sometimes complete texts are sent to the author through CIA agents in the Information Service.

Visits to India by American specialists in international affairs, social and economic problems, literature and the arts are arranged by the CIA. They lecture at universities and colleges. The majority are CIA agents and are sent to India for some special purpose. For instance, the CIA using the USIS as cover, organized a trip for a CIA agent. He was the well-known American author, Luis Fisher[73] who was charged with the mission of influencing Indian Government circles where he was known as the author of a book about Gandhi. The number of such specialists visiting India with directives from the CIA has been growing from year to year.

It's an absolute fact that USIS employees in the interests of the CIA made use of representatives of Indian business circles who held influential positions in the country's legislative and executive organs. Some of those cooperating with the USIS – actually the CIA – include Kamalnayan, a prominent industrialist in Bombay, Jogendra Singh, the representatives of large industrialists in parliament, and the Maharajah of Orissa, Prator Kashari Deo.[74] It seems

---

[71] Francis Robert Moraes (1907-74) was editor of several newspapers in India, including *The Indian Express*. Moraes authored numerous books: *The Revolt in Tibet* (1960); *Report on Mao's China* (1954); *Behind the Bamboo Curtain* (1956); *On the Chinese Communist Government* (1956); and *Jawaharlal Nehru: A Biography* (1956).

[72] Chandigarh is a city and a union territory in northern India. It serves as the capital of the states of Haryana and Punjab.

[73] Smith often misspells names. Louis Fischer (1896-1970) was an American journalist who wrote following books: *The Life of Mahatma Gandhi* (1950), which was the basis for the 1982 film *Gandhi*. He also wrote *The Life of Lenin* (1964), *The God that Failed* (1949), and *The War in Spain* (1937).

[74] Smith misspelled his name. "Pratap Keshari Deo (Bhawanipatna)" (1919-2001) as the Ruler (Maharaja) of Kalahandi (1939-47), Vice-President of the Eastern States Union (1947), and President of Ganatantra Parishad (1954-55/1959-60).

paradoxical that the USIS extends its contacts with such peculiar social groups as the maharajahs.

The US Information Services collaborated with a number of leading figures of the ruling party, the "Indian National Congress."[75] I know from conversation I had with the USIS had close ties with Ram Subhag Singh,[76] Secretary General of the Parliamentary group of the National Congress Party. Sadiq Ali was also in the same category.[77]

Leo Gentner,[78] a CIA agent was stationed in India from 1956 to 1958 and was responsible for financing agents, dirty propaganda, and subversion. He had an important post in the Embassy. During the war he was with the Price Control Board[79] in Washington. It was quite evident that economics and finance were not his strong points. He admitted once that he didn't have much time to devote to price control duties! Gentner spent several years after the war in Honolulu in the Hawaiian Islands.

Through its agents in USIS, the American Intelligence established close ties with the President of the Swatantra Party,[80] Ranga[81] and Party bosses, such as Masani.[82]

With every passing year the USIS extends its dirty work in India and collaborations more closely with the American Intelligence Services. These secret partners resort more frequently to methods of provocation, spread alarming rumours, and sow mistrust and bitterness among various groups of the population. The US Information Service paid some Indian papers for publishing slanderous material about some outstanding Indian leaders. One paper in collaboration with the CIA and USIS published articles, demanding the resignation of Krishna Menon,[83] India's Defense Minister. This was done with the plan of replacing him with an individual with pro-American leanings.

Therefore it would be nearer the truth to interpret the initials USIS as the United States Intelligence Service instead of United States Information Service. The former is more in keeping with the role of the USIS in India as an appendage to the CIA.

---

[75] One of the oldest and largest political parties in India.

[76] Ram Subhag Singh (1917-80) was an Indian politician, who was a member of the Indian National Congress political party, and also participated in the Indian independence movement.

[77] Sadiq Ali (1952-2011) was a senior politician of Kashmir. He was an elected legislator in the Kashmir State Assembly.

[78] Leo Gentner is mentioned in The Association for Diplomatic Studies and Training Foreign Affairs Oral History Project: Ambassador William C. Sherman, Interviewed by Thomas Stern (October 27, 1993).

[79] US Office of Price Administration. Not a CIA organization.

[80] The Swatantra Party was an Indian conservative political party from 1959 to 1974.

[81] N.G. Ranga (1900-95) was an Indian freedom fighter, parliamentarian, and farmer leader.

[82] Minocher Rustom "Minoo" Masani (1905-98) was an Indian politician and a leading figure of the Swatantra Party.

[83] V. K. Krishna Menon (1896-1974) was an Indian nationalist, diplomat and statesman, described as the second most powerful man in India by *Time* magazine after his ally and friend, Jawaharlal Nehru. Served as Minister of Defence (1957-62). Was often vilified in the Western press, including *Time* magazine, as a "snake charmer" and "Nehru's evil genius." Served as India's Ambassador to the United Nations (1952-62) and Indian High Commissioner to the United Kingdom (1947-52).

***

I resigned from the United States Government service in 1960 and left for Australia. Now I could observe events in India from a long distance as I no longer participated in that dirty game. However, the game continued. After the general elections to the Indian Parliament which took place two years later, I came across a pamphlet which had been published in the Indian city of Lucknow.[84] Its title was "US Interference in India's Elections." It concerned the subversive activities of the CIA in which I participated at one time. I recalled Harry Rozitske, Jack Curran, and dozens of other American agents engaged in subversion against the Indian nation.

The pamphlet stated that India's Minister of Internal Affairs has adequate proof of the interference of my former colleagues in the pre-election campaign. The central figure was none other than the First Secretary of the US Embassy in Delhi, Harry Rozitske. Actually he was a CIA chief and the person who instructed me in espionage activities. Nehru's government demanded that he leave India immediately.

Harry Rozitske was forced to leave India. The American Ambassador, Galbraith,[85] was told that if Rozitske didn't leave, he would be officially declared persona non grata[86] and the affair would reach scandalous proportions. Rozitske's aide, Cogan, an Embassy employee, was sent out with him.

These spies left India, but not without a little help from me. After leaving my official United States Government duties I revealed to the Government of India some facts about the activities of CIA against the country which I had grown to love during the many pleasant years I spent working there.

I wrote a revealing letter and sent it to India's Head of State.

In my letter I told about the activities of Harry Rositske and his partners in crime and about the big agents of CIA in the Indian Army Headquarters – General Bannerjee, General Thimmaya, Col. Sen. – I revealed what I knew. I did not give my return address and I don't know whether my letter reached the addressee. However, I think the letter was received because the people I mentioned were removed from their duties. I was glad that I could render the Indian people some real help.

By the time the CIA's activities in India were world-wide knowledge. *Time*, the American magazine wrote that the United States had spent 2,400,000 dollars in India. The money was spent to undermine Nehru's position. He championed India's stand on neutrality and had an aversion for the puppets placed on the dictator's thrones in some Asian and African countries.

After Nehru's death, the US Central Intelligence Agency turned its attention to Krishna Menon whom they had been trying to undermine for some time. He was the great statesman's associate and friend. The CIA methodically went about from one election to another in preparing the ground to remove Menon from the political scene. I had been told about this long-term operation as far back as the fifties. In 1958 I was a witness and a participant in that campaign and later observed how it developed. The pamphlet about US interference in the

---

[84] Lucknow is the capital city of Uttar Pradesh, India.

[85] **John Kenneth Galbraith (1908-2006) was a US economist and diplomat who served as the US Ambassador to India (1961-63).**

[86] **Persona Non Grata (PNG) means "an unwelcome person" and refers to the status of a foreigner who has been ejected from or not allowed into a country. Often referred to as being "pinged" for political reasons.**

general election in India revealed another new phase of the CIA's subversive activities against Krishna Menon.

The interference of the United States in the elections in Northern Bombay where Krishna Menon was the candidate, were crude and brutal. In the campaign against Menon, the CIA agents recruited plotters from the semi-fascist parties and groups, reactionary politicians and the anti-Socialist press. Morever just before the elections the American press began a campaign against Menon. *Time* magazine in the United States put out a special edition with a caricature of Krishna Menon on the cover. The edition was widely distributed in Bombay.

During that period many of my CIA friends were still working in India. I could probably name those who took part in the campaign to discredit Krishna Menon. However, I will present only the facts that were published in India. It was stated plainly that Robert E. Boies,[87] the US Consul in Bombay, covered the whole city in his limousine with consular license plates, handing out sums of money to his men in the polling stations. Colonel Robert Burrows,[88] on the military attache's staff, was conspicuous at that time by his unusual activity.

The chief American representative in the World Youth Assembly[89] who constantly travels by air from one country to another, spent an entire month in Bombay campaigning for Acharya Kripalani,[90] Menon's rival. A week before the elections, Watkinson of the American Technical Mission in Delhi, Leonard Sedman,[91] an Embassy attaché and Miss Stillwell moved to Bombay in order to carry out special CIA assignments. Arther Shhlesinger[92] arrived in India at that time to lecture, stirring up hatred of Krishna Menon. I suspect his activities were directed by the CIA.

That year the attempts to undermine Menon at the elections were unsuccessful. He won the election. Consequently the US Intelligence Service provided additional funds running into thousands dollars to be used until the final goal of ousting Menon was achieved. At the general elections in the Spring of 1967, Krishna Menon was finally blackballed.

---

[87] Robert E. Boies (1921-2014), graduated Yale University (1942), served as a reconnaissance officer in the First Marine Division and was in the Peleliu and Okinawa invasions during World War II where he was awarded the Purple Heart and Bronze Star. Returned to Yale to earn a Masters, and then a PhD in Eastern European History from Charles University in Prague. As a CIA operations officer, he served in Europe, South Asia, and the Middle East. He taught courses in East European History at George Mason University and the School of International Service at The American University. According to the 1973 US State Department Biographic Register: foreign affairs officer in the Department of Army (1949-59); US State Department in Bombay as a political officer (1959-62); Beirut as political officer (1962-64); and Rome as a political officer (1969) [these State Dept. listings are most likely CIA covers].

[88] Burrows is mentioned in Pauly V. Parakal's 1984 anti-CIA book, *Secret Wars of CIA*.

[89] World Assembly of Youth (founded 1949) is the international coordinating body of national youth councils and organizations.

[90] J. B. Kripalani (Acharya) (1888-1982) was an Indian politician, noted for holding the presidency of the Indian National Congress during the transfer of power in 1947. He was a Gandhian Socialist, environmentalist, mystic, and independence activist.

[91] It is remotely possible Smith has confused and misspelled his name. Could be "Leonard Seidman Unger" (1917-2010), US Ambassador to Laos (1962-64), US Ambassador to Thailand (1967-73), and the last US Ambassador to the Republic of China/Taiwan (1974-79).

[92] Smith clearly is referring to the noted historian and diplomat Arthur M. Schlesinger, Jr., though he mangles his name.

***

CIA's interference was quite evident when the Indian press published the news of the attempt on the life of Kamaraj,[93] president of the National Congress Party. The assassination attempt had been organised by the RSS Party.[94] Aware of their close ties with the CIA, it wasn't difficult for me to discern the work of my former colleagues.

On the seventh of November 1966 RSS party organized a massive demonstration against the progressive forces of India.

The wave of people reached the parliament where a short meeting was held. Then the RSS members led the excited crowd to the homes of ministers and political figures their party objected to. On the way the mob overturned and set cars ablaze, smashed windows, broke into homes. This was the way they gave vent to their despair brought about by privation and hunger. The instigators blamed Kamaraj and the other progressives for the people's misfortune. The reactionaries made clever use of the rebellious, starving mob in removing those who stood in their way.

The enraged mob stopped at the home of Kamaraj. About two hundred of them armed with knives and screaming "death to Kamaraj" hurled themselves over the fence onto the territory of the mansion. Kamaraj escaped through a back door and the raging mob wrecked his home.

Nanda,[95] the Minister for Internal Affairs was blamed for the incident. He was forced to resign. Who was interested in Nanda's resignation?

It seems to me that Nanda had discovered some of the deals involving the CIA and began to get to the bottom of things.

So it was necessary to make him harmless and that is exactly what happened. Of course, with the help of the Americans. Large sums of money had been necessary to organize such a demonstration and feed those who took part in it.

Incidentally, the United States makes no attempt to conceal that it spends large sums of money expressly for interference in India's internal affairs. As recently as June 13, 1967, the *New York Times* stated that "the CIA helped the right wing during the elections in India." Joseph Lelivelt[96] reported from Delhi that the Indian Government investigated the CIA's activities during the elections and discovered that the USA had contributed large sums of money to the

---

[93] Kumarasami Kamaraj (1903-75) was an Indian politician from Tamil Nadu. Known as the "Kingmaker" in Indian politics during the 1960s. He was the chief minister of Tamil Nadu (1954-63) and a Member of Parliament (1952-54/1967-75). He was involved in the Indian independence movement. As the president of the Indian National Congress, he was instrumental in navigating the party after the death of Jawaharlal Nehru and bringing to power his daughter Indira Gandhi as Prime Minister in 1966.

[94] Rashtriya Swayamsevak Sangh (RSS) Party is a right-wing charitable, educational, volunteer, Hindu nationalist, and non-governmental organization. It is the world's largest voluntary non-governmental organization. Its ideology is based on the principle of selfless service to India.

[95] Gulzarilal Nanda (1898-1999) was an Indian politician and economist who specialized in labor issues. He was the Prime Minister of India for two short periods following the deaths of Jawaharlal Nehru in 1964 and Lal Bahadur Shastri in 1966.

[96] Smith misspelled his name. "Joseph Lelyveld" (born 1937) was a *New York Times* journalist. He wrote the 2011 book, *Great Soul: Mahatma Gandhi and His Struggle With India*.

right-wing parties and their candidates. The Jan Sangh[97] and Swatantra parties received the largest contributions.

The *New York Times* report caused an upheaval in the Indian press. The papers published the debates that took place in Parliament on the subject. The deputies demanded an explanation from the Minister for Internal Affairs, Chavan.[98] The Minister replied that India's Investigation Bureau had enquired into CIA's activities during the elections. However, the results were not divulged to Parliament.

* * *

Allen Dulles, head of the CIA for many years, once stated that the whole world served as an arena for American espionage activities. This is quite true. It is my confirmed opinion that the CIA's activities in India cover just part of its vast network. After leaving India I kept track of the CIA agents I had worked with in order to discover where they continued their activities. It became apparent that they spread all over the world like the teeth of the legendary dragon, giving rise to evil. They are numerous. Only one out of five members of US embassies' staffs are real diplomats. The others are espionage agents.

Many of the intelligence agents that I knew very well in India are now in other countries. Edward Marelius,[99] with whom the reader is familiar, entrenched himself in neutral Sweden, under the cover of First Secretary in the US Embassy in Stockholm. John Waller carried out espionage in the Sudan. He was given the post of attaché in the US Embassy in Khartoum.[100] David Burgess became the director of the Peace Corps in Jakarta. Also with him in Jakarta is James Burns, Second Secretary of the Embassy.

The head of the CIA in Pakistan, Seymour Russel[101] is now in Italy. Robert Anderson who was a CIA agent in India not so long ago was Second Secretary of the US Embassy in Paris. William Grimsley[102] is now with the CIA in Delhi, and Harold Milks[103] and Knox are also agents

---

[97] Bharatiya Jana Sangh was an Indian nationalist political party (1951-77) and the political arm of Rashtriya Swayamsevak Sangh (RSS), a Hindu right-wing organization. In 1977, it merged with several other parties opposed to rule of the Indian National Congress and formed the Janata Party. After the Janata Party split in 1980, it was re-formed as the Bharatiya Janata Party, which is today one of India's largest political parties.

[98] Yashwantrao Balwantrao Chavan (1913-84) was the first Chief Minister of Maharashtra after the division of Bombay State and the fifth Deputy Prime Minister of India. He was popularly known as "Leader of Common People" and advocated social democracy and established farm co-operatives in Maharashtra.

[99] Possibly "Edward A. Marelius" who served as a US State Department attaché in Costa Rica.

[100] The capital of Sudan, Africa.

[101] Smith misspelled his name. "Seymour Russell" (died 2000) was a CIA officer who retired in 1973. After serving four years as a military intelligence officer in Italy, Russell joined the newly founded CIA (1947), serving in foreign and domestic posts for 26 years. As a member of the Clandestine Services, he served as Station Chief in Rome, Italy (1966-71) and in Karachi, Pakistan. He was also Deputy Chief in Athens, Greece, and Trieste, Italy, and Director of the CIA's Technical Services Division. See also: 1969 U.S. State Department. Biographic Register, Mader's 1968 anti-CIA propaganda book, *Who's Who In CIA*, and John Marks 1980 book, *The Search for the "Manchurian Candidate": The CIA and Mind Control*.

[102] William C. Grimsley. According to the 1973 U.S. State Department. Biographic Register: Grimsley (born 1927), graduated Columbia University (1951), served in the US Navy (1945-46), economics affairs officer for the Department of the Army (1955-56), joined the US State Department and served in Kabul, Afghanistan, as an economic assistant (1952), New Delhi (1956-62), then Kathmandu as an executive assistant (1967-73), and Japan (1977-79). See also Philip Agee's 1978 book, *Dirty Work: The CIA in Western Europe*; Kenneth Conboy's 2002 book,

who under the cover of journalists left the country recently.

Agents that I had known very well are now continuing their work in all parts of the world. As a I observed ascent of my former colleagues on the ladder of success, I know that each rung of their promotion represents stolen secrets, successful bribery, deception and even murder.

After India I was sent to Austria. For some time I worked in the American Embassy in Vienna. I was surprised that the network of the CIA in Austria in comparison with India is disproportionally large.

I consider it my duty to the American people to expose and hinder the activities of the Central Intelligence Agency.

END

The CIA's Secret War in Tibet; Julius Mader's 1988 anti-CIA book, *CIA-Operation Hindu Kush*; Mader's 1968 anti-CIA book, *Who's Who in CIA*.

[103] Harold K. Milks was an Associated Press correspondent whose many adventures included Cuba during the Bay of Pigs invasion. As chief of Caribbean Services, Milks, a veteran war correspondent and former Moscow bureau chief, ran the bureau from May 1959 until the spring of 1961. See: Jack Anderson's 1999 book, *Peace, War, and Politics: An Eyewitness Account*.

TARGET: ZHOU ENLAI

Publication: *Far Eastern Economic Review*
Published: 13 July 1995
Article: "Target: Zhou Enlai - Was America's CIA working with Taiwan agents to kill Chinese premier?"
Author: Wendell L. Minnick

It has been the plot of a hundred spy novels: a plane full of passengers is bombed to kill one man. In April 1955, that man was Chinese Premier Zhou Enlai[104] and the plane was Air-India's Kashmir Princess. However, unlike a spy yarn, the assassins missed their target and killed a planeload of passengers in vain.

New information uncovered by Oxford University scholar and Hong Kong native Steve Tsang, from British, Taiwanese, American and Hong Kong archives -- revealed in a recent *China Quarterly* article -- names Kuomintang[105] agents in Taiwan as the culprits. Though Tsang says

---

[104] **Zhou Enlai (1898-1976) was China's first Premier, serving from 1949 until his death in 1976. A skilled and able diplomat, Zhou served as the Chinese foreign minister from 1949 to 1958. Advocating peaceful coexistence with the West after the Korean War, he participated in the 1954 Geneva Conference, and helped orchestrate US President Richard Nixon's visit to Beijing.**

[105] **The Chinese Nationalist Party (KMT) lost the Chinese Civil War and was forced to rebase on the island of Taiwan in 1949.**

that the United States Central Intelligence Agency was not involved, questions persist.

On the night of April 11, 1955, the chartered Air-India flight was carrying a minor delegation of Chinese and East Europeans from Hong Kong to Indonesia to attend the Afro-Asian Conference in Bandung. Around 7 p.m., at 18,000 feet, a time bomb detonated in the wheel bay of the starboard wing, blowing a hole in the No. 3 fuel tank. The crew heard the explosion, the fire-warning light for the baggage compartment came on, and horrified passengers watched the fire travel up the wing. The captain shut off the right inboard engine, fearing it would catch fire, leaving the other three engines running. The crew sent out three distress signals giving their position over the Natuna Islands before the radio went dead.

Before the radio failed, the Jakarta control tower asked if Chinese Premier Zhou Enlai was aboard. The answer was no, but the question must have bewildered the crew. Unknown to them, Zhou was the very reason they were now fighting for their lives.

Zhou's travel plans were kept in strict secrecy. In fact, the premier did not leave China until April 14 -- three days after the bombing -- when he flew to Rangoon to meet with Indian Prime Minister Jawaharlal Nehru and Burmese leader U Nu before continuing on to Bandung.

The secrecy that surrounded Zhou's travel plans saved his life -- and doomed the Kashmir Princess. The same Air-India plane was scheduled to fly to Rangoon to pick up Zhou for his trip to Indonesia. In fact, Tsang argues Zhou knew about the assassination plot.

"Evidence now suggests that Zhou knew of the plot beforehand and secretly changed his travel plans, though he did not stop a decoy delegation of lesser cadres from taking his place," Tsang wrote in the September 1994 issue of the academic journal, *China Quarterly*.[106]

The Kashmir Princess was only an hour from its scheduled landing in Jakarta when the captain decided to ditch the plane at sea. The crew issued life jackets and opened the emergency doors to ensure a quick escape. As the cold wind rushed into the plane, the aircraft began the descent into the dark waters below.

The starboard wing struck the water first, tearing the plane into three parts. The flight engineer, navigator and first officer escaped. But the remaining 16 passengers and crew members died, including seven Chinese cadres, mainly journalists, and three journalists from Austria, Poland and North Vietnam.

Rumours of CIA and KMT involvement surfaced immediately. The day after the crash, China's Foreign Ministry issued a statement that described the bombing as "a murder by the special service organizations of the United States and Chiang Kai-shek," the head of the KMT government.

Zhou was a constant irritant to the CIA and KMT during this time. The CIA's covert war with China was in full swing during the 1950s. The agency created several front organizations to deal with Communist expansionism in Asia. These included the Asia Foundation,[107] Civil Air Transport (later renamed Air America)[108] and the *China Quarterly*.

Many in the West saw the Bandung conference as a gathering of communists and pro-communists. The CIA believed that China planned to use the conference to boost its image as a world power. In response, the agency sent agents posing as journalists to cover the conference. Some CIA officers may have had other ideas.

---

[106] Tsang, Steve, "Target Zhou Enlai: The 'Kashmir Princess' Incident of 1955," *China Quarterly* (September 1994), No. 139, 766-782.

[107] Smith, Joseph, *Portrait of a Cold Warrior: Second Thoughts of a Top CIA Agent* (NY: Ballantine Books, 1976).

[108] Leary, William, *Perilous Missions: Civil Air Transport and CIA Covert Operations in Asia* (Smithsonian Institution Press, 2002).

Eleven years later, a U.S. Senate committee[109] investigating CIA operations heard testimony that gave murky details of a CIA plot to assassinate an "East Asian leader" attending a 1955 Asian conference. The leader's identity remained under wraps for another 11 years. In 1977, William Corson,[110] a retired U.S. Marine Corps intelligence officer who served in Asia, published "Armies of Ignorance," identifying him as Zhou Enlai.

Corson told the Review that Gen. Lucian Truscott[111] had brought the operation to a halt. Soon after his appointment as the CIA's deputy director in 1954, Truscott discovered that the CIA was planning to assassinate Zhou. During the final banquet in Bandung, a CIA agent would slip a poison into Zhou's rice bowl that would not take effect for 48 hours, allowing for Zhou's return to China. According to Corson, Truscott confronted CIA Director Allen Dulles, forcing him to terminate the operation.

Tsang found evidence in archives that points directly to KMT agents operating in Hong Kong as the perpetrators of the plane bombing. According to him, the Nationalists had a special-operations group stationed in Hong Kong responsible for assassination and sabotage. Designated the Hong Kong Group under Maj-Gen Kong Hoi-ping, it operated a network of 90 agents.

"The specific team actually behind this attempt to assassinate Zhou Enlai was the Number Five Liaison Group under Tsang Yat-nin," the Oxford scholar said. "In this operation, Tsang was under the command of Wu Yi-chin" of the KMT's Security Bureau.

In March 1955, the KMT's Tsang recruited Chow Tse-ming, alias Chou Chu, who had been a cleaner for Hong Kong Aircraft Engineering Co. since 1950. Chow's job at the airport gave him easy access to the Air-India plane. The Nationalists offered Chow the then-fantastic sum of HK$600,000 (currently $78,000) and refuge in Taiwan, if necessary.

The plane flew from Bombay to Hong Kong, and was grounded for 80 minutes to allow for refuelling and boarding. At this time, Chow placed the bomb on board. At 1:30 p.m., the Air-India plane made its last take-off, crashing hours later.

On May 26, an Indonesian board of inquiry announced that a time bomb with an American-made MK-3 timer/detonator was responsible for the crash. The revelation triggered political shock waves in Hong Kong. The governor, Sir Alexander Grantham,[112] had already announced that his office was satisfied no tampering had occurred in Hong Kong.

The Hong Kong authorities offered HK$100,000 for information leading to the arrest of

---

[109] U.S. Senate, Final Report of the Select Committee to Study Governmental Operations With Respect to Intelligence Activities, Supplementary Detailed Staff Reports on Foreign and Military Intelligence. Book 4, *Alleged Assassination Plots Involving Foreign Leaders*, 94th Congress, Second Session, S. Rept. 94-755 (April 23, 1976), 132-133.

[110] William R. Corson, 74, a retired lieutenant colonel in the Marine Corps and expert on counterinsurgency warfare died in 2000. For much of his career, Corson was an intelligence officer on special assignment with the CIA and the US Marine Corps. He wrote numerous non-fiction books on intelligence and Vietnam: *Consequences of Failure* (1973), *The Armies of Ignorance: The Rise of the American Intelligence Empire* (1977), *The New KGB: Engine of Soviet Power* (1985); and *Widows* (1989).

[111] Lucian King Truscott, Jr. (1895-1965) was a highly decorated commanding officer in the European theater during WW II. 1951, he joined the CIA as "Special Consultant to the United States Commissioner" in Frankfurt, Germany. In 1953, President Eisenhower approved CIA Director Allen Dulles' recommendation that General Truscott be appointed the CIA's Deputy Director for Coordination, which gave him control of the CIA's network of agents. His responsibilities included facilitating the overthrow of governments in Iran and Guatemala. Truscott left the CIA in 1958.

[112] Alexander William George Herder Grantham (1899-1978) was a British colonial administrator who governed Hong Kong and Fiji.

those responsible. They questioned 71 people connected with the servicing of the Air-India flight. When police began to focus on Chow, he stowed away aboard a CIA-owned Civil Air Transport aircraft on a flight to Taiwan.

The Hong Kong police concluded that the KMT had recruited Chow to plant the bomb. Apparently, he had bragged to friends about placing it aboard the airliner. He had also spent large sums of money before he left Hong Kong. Police tried to extradite Chow; Taiwan refused to acknowledge him as a KMT agent.

But the story does not end with Chow's escape. On October 24, 1967, the Soviet newspaper *Pravda* announced the defection of an American, John Discoe Smith. In his memoirs, entitled "I Was an Agent of the CIA," published in *Literaturnaya Gazeta* that year, Smith detailed his adventures as an agent -- including his delivery of a time bomb to a Chinese Nationalist agent. He says that in 1955, Jack Curran, a CIA officer attached to the U.S. Embassy in New Delhi, asked him to deliver a bag to a Wang Feng [or Van Fen] at the Maidens Hotel in the Indian capital. Smith claimed it was a bomb, the one used to destroy the Air-India plane.

According to a 1979 classified U.S. Senate International Operations report, the KMT planned another assassination of Zhou Enlai in 1971, this time using a trained "kamikaze dog wearing a remote-controlled bomb." The plot, the report says, was as bizarre as it was elaborate. The KMT sent an agent to Switzerland to pay an Italian neo-fascist group to carry out the plan while Zhou was visiting Paris. KMT agents had acquired linens that Zhou had used in a hotel outside of China. They used them to train a police dog named Kelly to learn Zhou's scent. The dog was to be outfitted with a remote-control bomb, which would be detonated when Kelly made contact with Zhou. The KMT dropped the plan when China cancelled Zhou's trip.

The urbane Chinese leader later played an important role in reaching a détente between the U.S. and China, making the assassination attempts on Zhou's life now seem ironic.

END

AIR INDIA BOMBING AND ZHOU ENLAI

by

Wendell Minnick

Note to Reader: This is an unpublished report produced in the early 1990s based on my research on the Air India bombing.

Air India Passengers and Crew

Foreign Journalists:

Dr. Friedrick Jensen, a journalist working for the East Germany News Agency.
Mr. Jeremi Starec, working as a Polish journalist.
Vuong Minh Phuomg, a Vietminh delegate and journalist.

Chinese Delegates and Journalists:

Li Ping.
Hao Feng-ke (former Inner Mongolia official).
Chung Pu-yun.
Hung Tso-mei (head of New China News Agency or Xinhua in Hong Kong).
Tse Hung.
Li Chao-chi (former trade official in Hankow).
Shen Chien-tu.
Shih Chih-ang (#2 man of Beijing's Chief Foreign Purchase Agency).

Crew:

Commander, Captain D.K. Jatar.
Flight Officer, Captain M.C. Dixit (survived crash).
Ground Engineer, Mr. A.S. Karnik (survived crash).
Navigator, Mr. J.C. Patak (survived crash).
Flight Engineer, K.D. Cunha.
Purser, Mr. D. Souza.
Assistant Purser, Mr. Pimenta.
Air Hostess, Miss Gloria Berry.

"EAST ASIA LEADER"

In 1955, twenty-nine Asian and African nations were scheduled to meet in Indonesia at the Bandung Conference to discuss a variety of trade and security issues. China would use the conference in an attempt to open talks with the United States and boost China's image as a world power.

Officially, China proposed that the members of the conference subscribe to what Chinese officials referred to as the "five principles" of coexistence – respect for territorial integrity and sovereignty, non-aggression, non-interference in each other's internal affairs, equality and mutual benefit, and peaceful coexistence.

Premier and Foreign Minister Zhou Enlai, China's chief delegate, was scheduled to attend with an impressive delegation, including Cabinet Vice Premier General Chen Yi, Foreign Trade Minister Yeh Chi-chuang, Vice Foreign Minister Chang Han-fu, and China's Ambassador to Indonesia Huang Chen.[113]

Zhou was one of China's most gifted international diplomatists and one of China's best leaders. Educated in Japan, Germany, and France, Zhou was the practical organizer and administrator that breathed life into Mao Zedong's theoretical ideas.

Zhou's trip outside China could have been a tempting target for the Central Intelligence Agency (CIA) and the Kuomintang (KMT or Chinese Nationalist Party).

In 1976, testimony given during a U.S. Senate Committee investigating CIA operations gave murky details of a CIA plot to assassinate an "East Asian leader" planning to attend an unnamed conference in 1955:

> The Deputy Chief testified that during his tenure at a CIA station in Asia, where he served after PB/7 was disbanded, he sent a cable to headquarters from the station outlining a proposed media propaganda program. He later learned that the other station officers had attached an additional paragraph to his cable suggesting that an East Asian leader should be assassinated to disrupt an impending Communist conference in 1955.
>
> A reply cable was received immediately from CIA headquarters disapproving the recommendation to assassinate the East Asian leader. According to the Deputy Chief, the cable "strongly censured" the Station and indicated "in the strongest possible language this Agency has never and never will engage in any such activities." The cable added: "immediately proceed to burn all copies of any documents relating to this request." The Deputy Chief testified that a senior representative from CIA headquarters arrived shortly at the station to reprimand the officers involved in the incident.[114]

---

[113] Szulc, Tad, "Burma Kept Waiting for Arrival of Chou," *New York Times* (April 14, 1955), 1, 10.

[114] U.S. Senate, Final Report of the Select Committee to Study Governmental Operations With Respect to Intelligence Activities, Supplementary Detailed Staff Reports on Foreign and Military Intelligence. Book 4, *Alleged Assassination Plots Involving Foreign Leaders*, 94th Congress, Second Session, S. Rept. 94-755 (April 23, 1976), 132-133.

The unidentified "deputy chief" once served under Boris Pash, who headed the CIA's Program Branch 7 (PB/7) until it was disbanded in 1952. PB/7 was the CIA's first assassination and kidnapping unit.[115] The fact that it was the former deputy chief of the CIA's assassination unit, who refers to an ambiguous assassination operation of an "East Asian leader," is curious and set about a great deal of speculation that the Air India bombing was possibly a CIA operation. However, most of the evidence points to direct involvement by the KMT on Taiwan.[116]

Despite PB/7's macabre charter, it reportedly never carried out any assassination or kidnapping operations before being dismantled.

The reference to the identity of the "East Asian leader" remained vague, but William R. Corson, a retired Marine Corps intelligence officer who served in Asia, and as an unofficial adviser to the Church Committee, identifies him as Zhou Enlai. According to Corson, General Lucien Truscott stopped the plan to assassinate Zhou Enlai. In 1954, President Eisenhower appointed Truscott as the CIA's deputy director for "Community Affairs."

Truscott previously served as the CIA's first station chief in West Germany in 1951 with 1,200 men under his command and previously served in China during World War II.[117]

Eisenhower was concerned about CIA Director Allen Dulles' impulse to use covert operations. Truscott was assigned to babysit Dulles and keep Eisenhower informed of CIA activities that might embarrass the United States. Officially, Truscott's role was that of mediator between the CIA and military intelligence services.

Soon after his appointment, Truscott discovered that the CIA was planning an elaborate assassination plot targeting Zhou Enlai. During the final banquet of the Bandung Conference, an indigenous agent would slip an undetectable poison into Zhou's rice bowl. The poison would not take effect for forty-eight hours, allowing for his return to China. According to Corson, Truscott confronted Dulles about the mission forcing him to terminate the operation.[118]

The CIA has experimented with a variety of poisons over the years. One of the most famous involved the extraction of a natural toxin from shellfish. Concentrated amounts equally two-tenths of a milligram, about the size of a pinhead, would kill a man in ten seconds. The CIA also studied ways of assassination by way of natural causes. In 1952, the CIA's Chemical Branch considered studying cancer and heart attack victims to learn of a method of introducing physiologically active chemicals to induce death by natural causes. As late as 1971, the CIA reportedly provided a sealed container carrying the African Swine Flu virus to a group of Anti-Castro terrorists who released it at a farm in Cuba. The Cuban government was forced to slaughter 500,000 pigs to stop the disease from spreading.[119]

---

[115] Corson, William, *The Armies of Ignorance* (NY: Dial/Wade, 1977), 363.

[116] I urge all researchers on this topic to read: Tsang, Steve, "Target Zhou Enlai: The 'Kashmir Princess' Incident of 1955," *China Quarterly* (September 1994), 766-782.

[117] Powers, Thomas, *The Man Who Kept the Secrets* (NY: Pocket Books, 1977), 171.

[118] Corson, 365-366.

[119] Burros, Marian, "CIA Toxin Related to Red Tide," *Washington Post* (September 19, 1975), A21; "CIA Considered Inducing Death," *Washington Post* (April 2, 1979), A2; Fetherson, Drew, and John Cummings, "CIA Linked to 1971 Swine Virus in Cuba," *Washington Post* (January 9, 1977), A2.

KASHMIR PRINCESS

Around 7:00 p.m. on Monday, April 11, 1955, a chartered Air India Constellation[120] airliner, dubbed the "Kashmir Princess," carrying a delegation of Chinese minor officials and journalists to the Bandung Conference, was at 18,000 feet when a time bomb detonated in the wheel bay of the starboard wing.[121]

The blast blew a hole directly into the number three fuel tank and another large hole into the baggage compartment. The crew heard a muffled explosion, and the fire warning light came on for the luggage compartment. Fire extinguisher units automatically switched on to no effect. The fire traveled down the wing. Captain Jatar feathered the right inboard engine, fearing it would catch fire, but left the outboard and two port wing engines running.

Smoke poured from the air ducts filling the cabin and cockpit. The hydraulic system failed and visibility from inside the cockpit deteriorated. The crew sent out three distress signals giving their position at 108 miles north of Kuching, Sarawak, over the Natuna Islands before the radio went dead. They were only an hour from their scheduled landing at Jakarta, but now it made no difference.

In Jakarta, the control tower managed to ask if Premier Zhou Enlai was aboard the aircraft. The answer was "no," but the question must have bewildered the crew frantically working to keep the plane under control. Unknown to them, Zhou was the very reason they were now fighting for their lives.

Zhou kept his travel plans secret late into the trip and went to Rangoon to meet with Egyptian President Gamal Abdel Nasser,[122] Indian Prime Minister Nehru,[123] and Burmese leader U Nu[124] before going to Bandung. The same plane was scheduled to fly to Rangoon to pick up

---

[120] The Lockheed Constellation ("Connie") is a propeller-driven, four-engine airliner built by Lockheed between 1943-58.

[121] "Air India Crash Caused by Time Bomb, Indonesian Court of Enquiry Reports," Taiwan-based *China Post* (May 28, 1955), 3; Rosenthal, A.M., "Chou Aides' Crash Held Due to Bomb," *New York Times* (May 27, 1955), 1, 6. According to Rosenthal's article, based on the Indonesian investigation commission's report, "the cause of this accident was an explosion of a timed infernal machine placed in the starboard wheel-well of the aircraft." Further, "a fire broke out in in the starboard wing and spread rapidly, causing failure in the hydraulic and electrical services." The aircraft began a "rapid descent" and the crew carried out emergency procedures for landing at sea "calmly" under "extremely difficult conditions." The aircraft hit the water with the starboard wingtip "while under partial loss of control and broke up on impact." The report said evidence of the bomb from the salvaging consisted of "(A) Bulging outward of the skin and strut members in the immediate area of the explosion. (B) A deep pitting by shrapnel of the skin and structural members facing the explosion. (C) A hole blown inward into the Number 3 fuel tank." The recovery included "four parts of a twisted, burned and corroded clockwork mechanism that has no relation to any equipment or structure on the aircraft."

[122] Nasser (1918-1964) was the second President of Egypt (1956-1970).

[123] Jawaharlal Nehru (1889-1964) was the first Prime Minister of India (1947-64).

[124] U Nu (1907-95) was the Burmese Prime Minister from 1948-1956, 1957-1958, and 1960-1962. Today, Burma is known as Myanmar.

Zhou and his delegation for a return trip to Indonesia.[125]

Air India was too far out at sea to make it to an airstrip, and Captain Jatar decided to ditch the plane at sea. The captain ordered the air hostess Gloria Berry and flight pursers Mr. D. Souza and Mr. Pimeta to issue life jackets to the passengers. The emergency doors were opened to ensure a quick escape. As the cold wind rushed into the plane, Air India began the descent into the dark waters below.

On a island only four miles away a group of workers on a coconut plantation watched the plane, bellowing smoke, descend into the sea. The plane landed in thirty feet of water about 100 miles from their last distress call off the coast of Borneo. The starboard wing struck the water first tearing the plane into three parts – the cockpit, cabin, and tail.

According to Steve Tsang, "The cabin, where the passengers were, sank immediately. The three survivors, all members of the crew, were in either the cockpit or the tail section."[126]

The Flight Engineer A.S. Karnik and Navigator J.C. Pathak were thrown out of the plane on impact through one of the open emergency exits, and First Officer M.C. Dixit managed to escape through the cockpit's storm window.[127] No one else survived the crash, resulting in the death of sixteen passengers and crewmembers.

HONG KONG: RESCUE AND INVESTIGATION

The plane had left Kai Tak Airport in Kowloon, Hong Kong, at 1:30 p.m. under tight security. The plane had flown in from Bombay, India, to Hong Kong, and was grounded for eighty minutes to allow for refueling and the boarding of passengers. Air India supervised every aspect of refueling and servicing.

A member of the crew remained on the plane at all times, and the China Travel Service (CTS), a proprietary of the People's Republic of China, supervised the handling of the passengers. CTS also delivered thirty-seven pieces of baggage to the plane and loaded them under Air India supervision. In addition, the CTS chartered the Air India aircraft.

The delegation arrived in Hong Kong by train from Beijing on Saturday and was accompanied to the Kai Tak airport by the Hong Kong police on Monday. The passengers were escorted directly to the plane by airline "motor bus" and Hong Kong authorities waved the usual customs and immigration formalities.[128]

The entire time the plane was on the ground at Kai Tak it was under Hong Kong police protection with a senior inspector in charge. No unauthorized persons were allowed near the plane. Members of the delegation entered the plane and it took off for Bandung without any difficulties.

The New China News Agency (Xinhua) notified the director of the Special Branch of Hong Kong police early on the day of Sunday, April 10, that eleven journalists and a Vietminh[129] delegate would also be traveling on the flight, but included no warning about any possible danger.

---

[125] "Search for Airliner," *South China Morning Post* (April 12, 1955), 1.

[126] Tsang, Steve, "Target Zhou Enlai: The 'Kashmir Princess' Incident of 1955," *China Quarterly* (September 1994), No. 139, 766-782.

[127] "Air India Statement," *South China Morning Post* (April 12, 1955), 1.

[128] "Airliner Bomb Inquiries," *London Times* (May 28, 1955), 6.

[129] Vietminh = League for the independence of Vietnam.

However, the acting head of the European Department of China's Foreign Ministry informed the British Chargé d'Affairs in Beijing, Humphrey Trevelyan,[130] the day before of a possible threat against the delegation by Chinese Nationalists (KMT). Trevelyan did inform Hong Kong authorities of a possible threat to the delegation. Additional security precautions were taken, but it was the Chinese government that handled the delegation in Hong Kong. Chinese officials kept their location, the name of the airline, and flight plan a secret until a day before the trip. This led to rumors that Zhou Enlai would be on the first Air India flight to Bandung.

Immediately following Air India's emergency call for help the British sent two Royal Air Force Sunderland Flying Boats and several ships, including the British freighter Silver Ash, into the area to search for survivors. The Singapore ship service sent out an urgent call to all ships in the area every half hour to search for survivors. The Indonesian Air Force also sent several aircraft into the area to search for survivors. It was an Indonesian patrol boat that finally spotted the wreckage.

The survivors swam eight hours in "Mae West"[131] life jackets to Sidanau Island four miles away, where they were given some minor medical attention at the small village of Tentent. They were later transferred from the 250-ton trawler *Taype*,[132] a local fishing boat, to the Royal Navy survey ship H.M.S. *Dampier*,[133] where they were treated for shock.

Air India officials, Mr. K.K. Menon, assistant divisional manager in Singapore, and Captain K. Vishwanath, divisional operations manager, chartered a plane and flew over the area of the crash, personally searching for survivors. They later were taken by boat to the crash site for a personal inspection.

The *Dampier* picked up the three survivors and three additional bodies. The captain, Commander Charles Roe, supervised the first initial inspection of the wreckage by four navy divers. Initially, nothing of substance was discovered that indicated foul play. The British divers who inspected the wreckage discovered the port wing sound, but the starboard wing had been ripped apart. The cockpit windows and wiper blades were still intact, but did discover a large hole behind the cabin in the fore part of the aircraft, probably the source of the fire from the baggage compartment. The ruckus caused three of the bodies to float to the surface, two of which were crew members, and the other was too damaged for immediate identification.

Despite the harrowing experience, the survivors were in reasonable condition and able to walk from *Dampier* when she docked in Singapore. There they were interviewed by British officials and entered a naval hospital for treatment. First Officer Dixit suffered a broken collarbone, Navigator Patak broke the bone in his left forearm, and Engineer Karnik had lacerations about his head.

The *Dampier* crew built roughly made coffins for the dead, setting them on the aft deck and

---

[130] Humphrey Trevelyan (1905-85) was a British diplomat and author. Served as British Chargé d'Affairs *ad interim* to the People's Republic of China (1953-55), Ambassador to Egypt (1955-56), Iraq (1958-61), and Soviet Union (1962-65).

[131] Mary Jane "Mae" West (1893-1980) was a popular Hollywood actress known for her sex appeal.

[132] There is some confusion as to the owner of the Taype. Some archival information indicates it was given to the Philippines and/or Singapore in 1945 as a freighter. Formerly a US Coast Guard "coastal freighter" (FS 284).

[133] HMS Dampier (K611/A303) was a Bay-class frigate of the British navy. Operational from 1948 to 1968 and based entirely in Singapore carrying out survey work.

covering each of them with a white ensign.[134] When the ship came into port Bosun's pipes were shrilled in salute as British sailors carried the coffins off *Dampier* and into closed naval ambulances in Singapore. Apparently, Indian Commissioner R.K. Tandon was emotionally moved by the act and thanked the British armed forces for their courtesy. Two of the bodies were later identified as Indian crew members, Flight Engineer K.D. Cunha and Assistant Purser Pimenta. The third body was not identified. The body of the Captain, D.K. Jatar, would not be found until May 2 still trapped in the cockpit.[135] In June 1955, the President of India, Dr. Rajendra Prasad, would bestow India's Gallantry Award to the surviving members and the five crew members killed.[136]

Since the plane crashed in Indonesian waters, Indonesian authorities handled the investigation at the crash site. However, separate criminal investigations would be conducted in Hong Kong and India.

CHARGE AND COUNTER-CHARGE

The Chinese government wasted no time in blaming both U.S. and Nationalist (KMT) agents of involvement in the destruction of Air India. The day after the crash, a Chinese Foreign Ministry statement accused the U.S. and Nationalist (KMT) agents of "murder." The Foreign Ministry also announced that they had information that there was a plot to sabotage that Air India plane.[137]

According to the Foreign Ministry, the warnings were communicated to the Chargé d'Affairs in Beijing, Humphrey Trevelyan, who does admit sending a cable to Hong Kong authorities about Beijing's concern that the "Nationalist might make trouble for a party of Chinese journalists when they left Hong Kong."[138]

The New China News Agency (Xinhua) stated, "secret agent organizations of the United States and Chiang Kai-shek succeeded in the plot…to murder members of the Chinese delegation headed by Premier Chou En-lai [Zhou Enlai] and sabotage the Asian-African conference."[139] Trevelyn protested the charge arguing that the Chinese only informed him verbally in a general way that the Nationalists (KMT) might cause problems for the delegation in Hong Kong. He insisted that Chinese officials were not specific with their accusations before the crash.[140]

---

[134] The White Ensign is a flag flown on British navy ships and consists of a red St. George's Cross on a white field with a Union Flag in the upper canton.

[135] "Body of Pilot Found," *South China Morning Post* (May 3, 1955), 11.

[136] "India Honors Air Crewmen," *New York Times* (June 19, 1955), 52.

[137] "Crash Report," *London Times* (April 25, 1955), 30; "Frenzied Outburst by Red China," *South China Morning Post* (April 17, 1955), 1, 8; "Peiping Charges Indian Airliner Sabotage," Taiwan-based *China Post* (April 14, 1955), 3; Ronan, Thomas P., "London Disputes Peiping on Crash," *New York Times* (April 18, 1955), 1, 4; "Survivor's Story of Air Crash," *South China Morning Post* (April 14, 1955), 1, 18.

[138] "London Disputes Peiping on Crash," *New York Times* (April 18, 1955), 1, 4.

[139] "Charge Concerning Airliner Resented," *South China Morning Post* (April 14, 1955), 1, 18.

[140] "Air Crash Protest by Peking," *London Times* (April 21, 1955); "British Move in Peking," *London Times* (April 28, 1955), 12.

The U.S. State Department reacted to the charges as outrageous propaganda. Senator Mike Mansfield (D., Mont),[141] a member of the U.S. Senate Foreign Relations Committee, went so far as to suggest that "dissident elements of the Chinese Communist Party" might have been responsible for the sabotage.[142]

An unsigned *New York Times* editorial reacted to China's accusation with the same demeanor:

> "It is vicious and is meant to be vicious. It is designed to fan the flames of the hate-America campaign in Red China. It is designed to provoke speculative questions among the 'neutral.' It is designed to put Red China in the role of the martyr at the opening of the Bandung Conference and to put the United States in the role of villain. This from the self-appointed apostle of 'co-existence.'"[143]

India's Communications Minister Jagjivan Ram[144] announced during a session of Parliament that India would participate in a separate inquiry into the crash. At one point, Speaker Ganesh Mavalankar[145] ruled another member out of order when he asked about China's charge that U.S. and Nationalist (KMT) agents were behind the crash of Air India.[146]

An Indian correspondent for the *Times of India* in Singapore covering the Indonesian investigation reported, "there were probably two explosions of the ill-fated aircraft – one in the baggage compartment and the other in the right wing panel."

Li Teh-chuan, the chairwoman of the Chinese Red Cross, announced during a speech on China Radio International ("Beijing Radio") on April 17 that Hong Kong was a "grave menace to China." Li claimed that within the past year, thirty-six Nationalist (KMT) fishing boats came to Hong Kong with explosives and Nationalist agents.[147] She continued by stating that Hong Kong authorities ignored their activities and allowed Nationalist (KMT) agents to infiltrate into mainland China from Hong Kong on sabotage missions. Li suggested Hong Kong was infested with Chiang Kai-shek agents.[148]

The relationship between Hong Kong and China has always been cumbersome and tricky.

---

[141] Michael Mansfield (1903-2001) served in the US House of Representatives (1943-53) and US Senate (1953-77). Served as US Ambassador to Japan (1977-88).

[142] Szulc, Tad, "Burma Kept Waiting," *New York Times* (April 14, 1955), 1, 10.

[143] "Peiping Vicious Nonsense," *New York Times* (April 15, 1955), 22.

[144] Jagjivan "Babuji" Ram (1908-86) was an Indian independence activist and politician from Bihar. He was also a Chamar caste member ("untouchable").

[145] Ganesh Vasudev Mavalankar (1888-1956), aka Dadasaheb, was an independence activist, the President of the Central Legislative Assembly from 1946-1947, then Speaker of the Constituent Assembly of India, and later the first Speaker of the Lok Sabha (the lower house of India's Parliament).

[146] "India Sets Inquiry on Loss of Airliner," *New York Times* (April 15, 1955), 3.

[147] Tsang, Steve, "Target Zhou Enlai: The 'Kashmir Princess' Incident of 1955," *China Quarterly* (September 1994), No. 139, 766-782.

[148] "Protest by Britain to China on Plane Crash," *South China Morning Post* (April 18, 1955), 1, 18.

The small British port has always viewed the relationship with China as delicate, given the sensitive location a Chinese invasion of Hong Kong, and turning off its fresh water supply in the north would be extremely easy. Threats by China, in any form, made Hong Kong authorities nervous. Officials quickly and repeatedly denied any possible sabotage of Air India while the plane was in Hong Kong.

However, part of the reason for the sabotage rumors was the fact that two rival unions worked at Kai Tak Airport – one was pro-Communist and the other pro-Nationalist (KMT). It was seen by many that one of these two groups may have been involved in the sabotage of the plane.[149]

However, Li was correct in her charge. Nationalist (KMT) agents used Hong Kong as a base for sabotage and espionage operations into mainland China throughout the 1950s and 1960s. According to Peer de Silva, the CIA's former Hong Kong station chief from 1962 to 1963, the Nationalists ran agents through Hong Kong on a regular basis. They would slip them into the Chinese traffic between Guangdong Province and Hong Kong. Once across the border, the agents would mingle with their fellow Chinese and set up intelligence networks.

Occasionally, the Hong Kong police would uncover a nest, and after a brief interrogation and incarceration, ship them back to Taiwan. De Silva found himself the brunt of British criticism of Nationalist espionage activities in Hong Kong due to the CIA's close relationship with Taiwan. De Silva commented on the problem: "Unscrambling these intelligence omelets was really more than human patience could endure."[150]

As one CIA veteran Joseph Smith observed in his autobiography:

> Hong Kong existed on the sufferance of the Chinese Communists. No more than a handful of saboteurs would be required to demolish the reservoir and parch the place out of existence, to name just one possibility, should the Chinese Communists ever become too annoyed by some operational prank of our [Chinese Nationalist] agents.[151]

Despite the cable from the British Chargé d'Affaires in Beijing, neither the New China News Agency (Xinhua) nor the China Travel Service (CTS), both quasi-official representatives of the People's Republic of China in Hong Kong, mentioned any possible trouble.

Zhou Enlai arrived in Rangoon, Burma, from Kunming, China, by air for a three-day visit on April 14 to meet with the Burmese Prime Minister U Nu, Egyptian Prime Minister Nasser, and Indian Prime Minister Nehru, a full three days after the crash of the Air India flight. Zhou's travel plans were kept in strict secrecy, for many believed Zhou was on the Air India flight in

---

[149] "Plane Crashes Enroute Bandung; Kills 15 Including 8 Peiping Delegates," Taiwan-based *China Post* (April 13, 1955), 1.

[150] De Silva, Peer, *Sub Rosa: The CIA and the Uses of Intelligence* (NY: Times Books, 1978), 194. His career can be traced back to World War II when he served in the US Army as a counterintelligence officer (1936-42). He also served as the chief of security during the making of the atom bomb at Los Alamos. In 1947, joined the CIA and served in the East European Division in Vienna, Austria (1956) and in 1959 served in Seoul, South Korea, as CIA station chief. In 1962 took over as station chief in Hong Kong. In 1963 became station chief in Saigon, South Vietnam, but was injured in a car bomb attack near the US Embassy and forced to return to the US in 1965. Retired in 1973.

[151] Smith, Joseph, *Portrait of a Cold Warrior: Second Thoughts of a Top CIA Agent* (NY: Ballantine Books, 1976), 138.

the first place. His arrival in Rangoon was a surprise to many. Even Burmese officials were kept in the dark. At one point, a Burmese reception committee went to the Mingaladon Airport in 96 degree heat to welcome him only to discover that the delegation had not arrived, but instead had crashed. What no one but a few knew was that the same Air India Constellation was scheduled to fly to Rangoon to pick up Zhou Enlai and the official delegation, after delivering the minor delegation (which crashed) of journalists and officials to Jakarta.

Ironically, Zhou might have met his end on another Air India airliner. When Zhou did depart Rangoon on an Air India Skymaster[152] airliner, it made a forced landing in Singapore after running into a severe storm.[153]

The Nationalists quickly denied the allegations. An unsigned commentary in the Taiwan-based *China Post*, in April, contained several interesting observations about the incident. First, the Communist government accused the Nationalists (KMT) of sabotage only thirty minutes after the announcement that Air India crashed. Secondly, if the Communists feared that Air India was unsafe on the ground in Hong Kong, why did it not arrange for refueling in Guangdong Province as it had in past trips? Thirdly, why did the Communists wait four days before sending representatives to the crash site? Fourth, the unsigned essay made the point of reminding the reader that the Communists were not beyond destroying a plane load of their own people for the sake of international sympathy; in other words, "elevating a few unwanteds to the rank of 'hero first-class' by involuntary martyrdom."[154]

The last point appears difficult to believe, but many who have studied Chinese history are familiar with the mysterious plane accidents of Dai Li (Tai Li)[155] and Lin Biao.[156] Another argument in favor of this theory is that the members on the plane were cadres of Gao Gang, who had been purged from his position in 1954 after an unsuccessful attempt to displace Zhou Enlai with himself. He was forced to commit suicide in August 1954 with poison.

The theory extends to trains. A group of five Chinese delegates, participating in the Marshall Mission[157] in Manchuria[158] and traveling by train, were stopped by "bandits" and

---

[152] Douglas C-54 Skymaster was a four-engine transport aircraft that was also used by the US Army Air Force in World War II and the Korean War. It also served as a presidential (Air Force One) aircraft during the 1950s.

[153] Szulc, Tad, "Chou Courts Nasser Before Asia Parley," *New York Times* (April 16, 1955), 1, 3.

[154] "Bandung Dead – Martyrs or Satyrs," Taiwan-based *China Post* (April 19, 1955), 4.

[155] **Dai Li** (1897-1946) studied at the Whampoa Military Academy, where Chiang Kai-shek served as Chief Commandant, and later became head of Chiang's Military Intelligence Service. He worked closely with the US military and intelligence services during World War II (Miles, Milton E., *A Difference Kind of War: The Unknown Guerrilla Forces in World War II China*, Taipei: Caves, 1986; and Yu, Maochun, *OSS In China: Prelude to Cold War*, Yale: 1996). Dai died in a plane crash on March 17, 1946, possibly arranged by his counterpart and rival Kang Sheng in the Chinese Communist Party (CPC). See also, Byron, John, and Robert Pack, *The Claws of the Dragon: Kang Sheng - The Evil Genius Behind Mao - And His Legacy of Terror in People's China*, Simon and Schuster, 1992.

[156] Lin Biao (1907-1971) was an important general in the Chinese Communist Party's army during the Chinese civil war with the KMT. However, during the 1960s, Lin became involved in the Chinese Cultural Revolution. When that soured, he and his family attempted to escape China, possibly to Russia, but the plane crashed killing everyone in Mongolia in September 1971. The Chinese government's official explanation is that Lin and his family attempted to flee following a botched coup against Mao Zedong.

[157] The Marshall Mission (December 1945-January 1947) was a failed diplomatic mission undertaken by US Army General George C. Marshall to China in an attempt to negotiate the unification of the Chinese Communist Party and the Chinese Nationalist Party (KMT) into a unified government.

executed. It was later learned that the five men had fallen out of favor with the Communist leadership and that the "bandits" were actually Communist agents.[159]

Though these arguments applied to the Air India bombing for conspiracy and political intrigue are interesting to speculate about, one had to be reminded of the location of these rumors. After all, any unsigned commentaries and articles coming from the Taiwan-based *China Post* in 1955 were probably the work of the CIA or the Chinese Nationalists (KMT).

WHO'S WHO AND WHY

Though neither Zhou Enlai nor his official delegation were on the plane, a few of the members of the minor delegation who perished are interesting to examine. The chief Chinese journalist was Shen Chien-tu, who covered the visit to China of British Opposition leader Clement Attlee[160] the previous year and believed to be the head of the New China News Agency (Xinhua). Li Ping was also a journalist for Xinhua who covered the Korean War from the Communist side. Li Chao-li was described as the third ranking member of the Chinese Foreign Ministry's Press Department. Hung Tso-mei was head of the Xinhua office in Hong Kong.

Representing the Warsaw Pact was Dr. Friedrich Jensen,[161] a fifty-year old Austrian-born surgeon and writer who worked for the East German News Agency.[162] Jensen had joined the Communist Party at the age of twenty-five and worked as a surgeon during the Spanish Civil War.[163] He later went to China and worked as a surgeon for the Communist Army until 1949, married a Chinese woman, and made China his home. Jensen translated Chinese poems into his native German, wrote several books, and began working as a correspondent for *Neues Deutschland*[164] in 1954. The other journalist, Jeremi Starec, was Polish, and his death drew loud complaints from the Polish Foreign Ministry to the British and Hong Kong governments, but little appears in newspaper accounts about his past.

The plane also carried Chinese diplomats, including Shih Chih-ang, the second ranking member of China's chief foreign purchasing agent. Little is known of Hao Feng-ke, but he may

---

[158] An area in the northeast of China that *now* also borders North Korea.

[159] "Airworthiness of Ill-Fated Plane Challenged by Pilot Before Flight," Taiwan-based *China Post* (April 15, 1955), 3; "Crash of Jakarta Bound Plane Seen Engineered by Reds Themselves," Taiwan-based *China Post* (April 15, 1955), 1.

[160] Clement Richard Attlee (1883-1967) was a British Labour Party politician who served as UK Prime Minister (1945-51) and Leader of the Labour Party (1935-55).

[161] Friedrich Albert Jensen (1903-55).

[162] Allgemeiner Deutscher Nachrichtendienst (ADN), which means "General German News Service."

[163] Spanish Civil War (1936-39) was waged between the Republicans, who were loyal to the democratically elected Spanish Republic and backed by the Soviet Union, and the Nationalists, a fascist rebel group led by General Francisco Franco and backed by Nazi Germany. Writers such as Ernest Hemingway (*The Fifth Column* and *For Whom the Bell Tolls*) and George Orwell (*Homage to Catalonia*) participated in the conflict and wrote about the Republican's vain attempt to reinstall a democratic government.

[164] "New Germany" was a national East German daily newspaper and the official mouthpiece of the Socialist Unity Party of Germany.

have been a former Inner Mongolia[165] official. Li Chao-chi was described as a former trade officer in Hankow.[166]

The difficulty in ignoring these individuals stems from the mistaken belief that they were unimportant minor officials. After all, Zhou Enlai was the target and numerous sources have pointed out that the New China News Agency (Xinhua) is and always has been a source of espionage for Chinese intelligence services. Hong Kong and Western intelligence sources quickly pointed out that Huang Tso-mei (Raymond Huang) was one of China's most important intelligence officers in Hong Kong. Huang once attended Hong Kong University and was well known for his pro-Communist activities going back before World War II. According to British sources, Huang was the "top Communist intelligence operative in this British colony post which he had held since end of the Pacific War."[167] Shih Chih-ang was also described as a Chinese intelligence officer. The two Warsaw Pact[168] journalists, Starec and Jensen, were both described as important propaganda agents for the Communists.[169]

It is a well-known fact in the intelligence community that the Chinese government overused the New China News Agency (Xinhua) as an intelligence tool, both as cover for intelligence officers and as a propaganda outlet. The fact that journalists are considered important propaganda agents should be no surprise. The CIA employed over four hundred journalists during the 1950s and 1960s as intelligence and propaganda agents.

CHOW TSE-MING: THE HUMBLE CLEANER

On May 26, a full month after the crash, the chairman of the Indonesian Board of Enquiry, R.J. Imawan, announced that a time bomb was responsible for the crash of Air India.[170] The announcement created shock waves in Hong Kong.

There was confidence in Hong Kong political and military circles that no saboteur could have reached the plane while it refueled in Hong Kong. Hong Kong's Governor, Sir Alexander Grantham,[171] already announced on April 20 that they were satisfied that no tampering

---

[165] Inner Mongolia Autonomous Region is in the northern section of China. Is considered "autonomous" but still under the control of the People's Republic of China.

[166] "11 Reds in Air Crash on Way to Parley," *New York Times* (April 12, 1955), 1, 7.

[167] "Reds Killed Are Intelligence Man and Journalists," Taiwan-based *China Post* (April 14, 1955), 1.

[168] Warsaw Pact (Treaty of Friendship, Co-operation, and Mutual Assistance) was created in response to the creation of the North Atlantic Treaty Organization (NATO). Both organizations were created for collective defense against aggression from either side. Warsaw made up Albania, Bulgaria, Czechoslovakia, East Germany, Hungary, Poland, Romania, and headed by the Soviet Union.

[169] "Crash Report," *Time* (April 25, 1955), 30; Red Reps Spies In Disguise," Special Correspondent; Taiwan-based *China Post* (October 28, 1955), 2; "Survivors of Crashed Indian Plane Picked Up," *South China Morning Post* (April 13, 1955), 1, 18.

[170] "Bomb in Airliner Wreck," *London Times* (May 27, 1955), 10; "H.K. May be Visited For Air Crash Enquiries," *South China Morning Post* (April 22, 1955), 1.

[171] Alexander William George Herder Grantham (1899-1978) was a British colonial administrator who governed Hong Kong and Fiji.

occurred in Hong Kong.[172] However, the discovery of the bomb, remnants still strapped to the rear outboard corner of the starboard wheelbay, could not be ignored.[173]

The commission consisted of three members of the Civil Aviation Department, a senior officer of the Indonesian Air Force, an official of Garuda Indonesian Airways, and a senior officer of the Indian Embassy. In mid-April, a large salvage ship from Singapore was sent to the sight of the wreck to raise it to the surface. The parts were taken to Pontianak, the West Borneo capital, where they were reassembled and studied.[174] The members of the commission flew to India and interviewed the survivors. They also visited Singapore and interviewed Commander Charles Roe, the captain of *Dampier*. The investigation was professional and thorough.

A summation of the investigation concluded that the "recovery of four parts of a twisted, burned and corroded clockwork mechanism that has no relation to any equipment or structure of the aircraft, found in the same area where the explosion took place, provided irrefutable evidence of an infernal machine's having been placed in this area.[175] No discussion of a second bomb surfaced as indicated by the *Times of India*, but given the damage to the baggage compartment the two bomb theory would be repeated over the years.

On May 27, Hong Kong authorities announced that everything would be done to bring those responsible to justice. Hong Kong police interviewed over one hundred people, but it was not until the official report gave the exact location of the bomb on the plane that helped Hong Kong police narrow the search to personnel with contact with that part of the plane. On June 12, Hong Kong authorities offered HK$100,000 for information leading to the arrest of those responsible.[176]

On August 2, Indian Prime Minister Jawaharlal Nehru announced that new information recently relayed by the Chinese government to Hong Kong authorities helped identify several suspects who were questioned by authorities. However, Nehru also announced that U.S. involvement seemed unlikely, going as far as criticizing China for attacking the U.S. without sufficient proof.

The Hong Kong police detained about twenty Chinese Nationals (KMT) who had direct and indirect connections with the servicing of the Air India plane. They were detained for a month while Hong Kong authorities deliberated on deporting them back to Taiwan.[177]

---

[172] "Hong Kong Reports No Plane Sabotage," *New York Times* (April 21, 1955), 2.

[173] *Hong Kong Annual Departmental Report by the Director of Civil Aviation for the Financial Year 1955-1956*, Section 8, "Aircraft Accidents," Number 62, Page 22: "An Air India International Constellation aircraft crashed into the sea off Sarawak on 11 April 1955 with the loss of 16 lives. The aircraft was partially salvaged and an investigation disclosed that it had been sabotaged by the insertion of a small time bomb in the port undercarriage compartment. The Director of Civil Aviation flew to Indonesia where the salvaged aircraft was subsequently taken to assist in the investigations." *Hong Kong Annual Report 1955*, "Colonial Office Statement on the Loss of the Air-India Aircraft 'Kashmir Princess'," Appendix I, South China Morning Post Library (January 11, 1956), 235-36. This last report is available at the back of this book in the Documents section.

[174] "Air India Crash Caused by Time Bomb, Indonesian Court of Enquiry Reports," Taiwan-based *China Post* (May 28, 1955), 3; "Hong Kong Reports No Plane Sabotage," *New York Times* (April 21, 1955), 2; "Indian Plane to be Raised," *New York Times* (April 22, 1955), 15; "New Peking Allegation Against H.K.," *South China Morning Post* (April 16, 1955), 18.

[175] Rosenthal, A.M., "Chou Aides' Crash Held Due to Bomb," *New York Times* (May 27, 1955), 1, 6.

[176] "Airliner Bomb Inquiries," *London Times* (May 28, 1955), 6; "Crash Arrests Denied," *New York Times* (August 4, 1955), 3; "Time Bomb in Airliner," *London Times* (June 13, 1955), 7.

[177] "Crash Arrests Denied," *New York Times* (August 4, 1955), 3; "Crash Suspects Held," *New York Times* (August

Hong Kong authorities questioned approximately seventy-one persons directly connected to the servicing of the Air India flight at Kai Tak Airport. Only twenty-seven had duties that placed them near the starboard wing. One of those individuals was cleaner by the name of Chow Tse-ming, an employee of the Hong Kong Aircraft Engineering Corporation. Chow, sometimes spelled Chau Tsz Ming, used two other alias: Chau Sik Kui and Chou Chu.

It was not until May 18 that Hong Kong police began focusing on Chow. Police could not find him at this home and later discovered that Chow had stowed away on a Civil Air Transport (CAT)[178] on a flight from Hong Kong to Taipei, Taiwan, on the same day.

A second suspect also escaped with Chow on the CAT flight. According to Steve Tsang, Chow was assisted by a colleague, Yu Pui to stow away in a little used luggage compartment on the CAT flight. "His escape did not seem to have been organized by KMT agents, as he was promptly arrested as an illegal immigrant at Taipei Airport, where the Immigration Officer intended to repatriate him to Hong Kong. However, once his real identity became known, the Taiwan authorities steadfastly refused all British requests to repatriate him to Hong Kong to stand trial, even after the British successfully enlisted the support of the United States."[179]

Police began questioning friends and relatives of Chow and discovered that he had been recruited by the Chinese Nationalists (KMT) to carry out the mission. Hong Kong authorities also found that on four separate occasions Chow did admit to friends that he had placed the bomb aboard Air India under orders of the KMT for a reward of HK $600,000.[180] Nationalist agents had given Chow a time-bomb that made a "slight ticking noise." Chow is also reported to have spent large sums of money after the crash, far beyond his financial means as a cleaner.[181]

A warrant was issued for his arrest, but the KMT government in Taiwan refused to return him to Hong Kong. No extradition treaty existed between Great Britain and Taiwan. No one else was charged with the crime. Taiwan at first stated that the stowaways were "refugees from the mainland who had simply passed through Hong Kong."[182] Civil Air Transport (CAT) officials acknowledged that one stowaway had been discovered in the baggage compartment upon arriving in Taipei, and that the individual had been taken into custody by authorities.

When inquiries were made of the man's identity, the authorities took the unusual step of refusing to discuss the matter. Spencer Moosa of the Associated Press complained of the silence:

3, 1955), 13; "Time Bomb in Airliner," *London Times* (June 13, 1955), 7.

[178] Leary, William, *Perilous Missions: Civil Air Transport and CIA Covert Operations in Asia* (Smithsonian Institution Press, 2002).

[179] Tsang, Steve, "Target Zhou Enlai: The 'Kashmir Princess' Incident of 1955," *China Quarterly* (September 1994), No. 139, 766-782.

[180] "Sabotage of Indian Airliner: Definite Information," *London Times* (August 3, 1955), 6; "UK Issues Statement on Responsibility of Air India Plane Crash," Taiwan-based *China Post* (January 12, 1956), 1, 4.

[181] "Chinese is Accused of Airliner Murders," *New York Times* (September 3, 1955), 2; "Crash of Jakarta Bound Plane Seen Engineered by Reds," Taiwan-based *China Post* (April 15, 1955), 1; "Nationalists Government Disclaims Knowledge," *South China Morning Post* (September 5, 1955), 1; "Sabotage of Indian Airliner: Formosa's Refusal to Return Suspect," *London Times* (January 11, 1956), 6; "Taipei Rebuffs British Request," *New York Times* (September 5, 1955), 2.

[182] "HK Police Get Warrant for Arrest of Aircraft Cleaner for Sabotage," Taiwan-based *China Post* (September 4, 1955), 1.

"The incident was so carefully hushed that it did not break in the newspapers here until a full week later."[183] When the stowaway story did break in Taiwan, many mistakenly believed that the stowaway was a Communist agent attempting to sneak into the country.

However, this rumor finally ended when Taipei authorities became indignant over Hong Kong's claims that the man was Chow Tse-ming. They later claimed that the two stowaways were arrested for illegal entry and that they were disillusioned Communist cadres who were escaping the mainland. However, authorities also refused to release their names, insisting that they were not connected in any way with the sabotage of Air India. An elaborate story was fed to the press describing how they had escaped from China through Macao then Hong Kong, but fearing assassination by Communist agents in Hong Kong, decided to escape to Taiwan.[184]

Today it is well-known that Civil Air Transport (CAT) was owned and operated by the CIA. CAT was later renamed Air America. It is difficult to believe that the two actually "stowed away" on the flight.

British frustration with the situation grew to a head in March 1956 during a debate in the British House of Commons when the Honorable John Baird[185] asked the Secretary of State for Foreign Affairs, Selwyn Lloyd,[186] what diplomatic channels the government was using in the extradition of Chow Tse-ming to Hong Kong. The debate became heated when Baird announced that the Americans had indirectly paid Chow the award, a sum in the equivalent of 40,000 British pounds, for placing the bomb aboard the plane.[187] Lloyd quickly came to the defense of the U.S. by stating that there was no positive evidence of American involvement. Baird's question certainly created doubt in many minds and as the decades followed the incident conspiracy theories grew.

MR. SMITH GOES TO MOSCOW

On October 24, 1967, the Soviet newspaper *Pravda*[188] announced that an American, John Discoe Smith, had defected to the Soviet Union and was writing his memoirs detailing his years as a "CIA agent." Smith published his memoirs in the English language edition of *Literaturnaya Gazeta*, entitled "I Was An Agent of the CIA."[189]

The Communist Party of India later published his memoirs as a propaganda tract. Smith was not a trained CIA officer, but a US State Department code clerk who became involved in

---

[183] Moosa, Spencer, "Plane Stowaway From Hong Kong Seen Linked to Air India Crash," Taiwan-based *China Post* (May 30, 1955), 4.

[184] "Gov't Says 2 Stowaway Fleeing Red Rule Not Connected With Air Crash," Taiwan-based *China Post* (May 31, 1955), 4.

[185] Baird (1906-65) was a member of the Labour Party.

[186] Lloyd served in this position from 1951-54.

[187] "Slander on U.S.," *London Times* (March 29, 1956), 4.

[188] *Pravda* is a Russian political newspaper associated with the Communist Party of the Russian Federation. During the Cold War it was the mouthpiece of the Communist Party of the Soviet Union.

[189] Anderson, Raymond, "Russians Say an Ex-CIA Man Who Spied in India Has Defected," *New York Times* (October 25, 1967), 17; "Memoirs of Former US Spy," *London Times* (November 3, 1967), 4; "Memoirs of US Secret Agent," *London Times* (October 25, 1967), 4; "US Defector Links CIA to '55 Air Crash," *New York Times* (November 22, 1967), 23.

courier duties for the CIA. Numerous operations are discussed and the names of several known CIA officers are mentioned. However, Smith also misidentifies many of the US State Department officials as being CIA.

A US State Department co-worker described him as a "communications technician, [who] fixed all the gadgets, the code machines."[190] Smith freely admits not being a CIA officer, but as a State Department employee recruited by the CIA while stationed in India. Smith was recruited first to obtain the codes of an unnamed developing country (possibly Morocco) that was drifting toward the Soviet bloc. Since communication clerks are either CIA officers or in close contact with them, Smith's contact with the CIA in New Delhi is likely true.

The main point that brings our attention to Smith is the fact that he mentions delivering a bomb to a Chinese Nationalist (KMT) named Van Fen (Wang Feng) in New Delhi. Smith recalled that he later learned that the bomb was used to destroy the Air India flight carrying the Chinese delegation to the Bandung Conference.

However, one might also conclude that the package Smith delivered to Wang Feng did not actually contain a time bomb. More than likely, if it carried anything, it contained a time delayed detonator. After all, the Nationalists were well endowed with bombs. They clearly did not need help from the CIA in that respect. The Indonesian investigation into the bombing did discover the remnants of a decide later identified as an US-made MK-3 timer/detonator.[191]

For those who differ from Smith's version of things, there is the matter of Smith's alleged mental instability. His wife described him as suffering from paranoia. According to his wife, Smith was ordered to return to the U.S. in late 1959 to consult a psychiatrist who diagnosed him as suffering from an acute stage of paranoia, thus forcing him to resign his position.

According to her divorce testimony, Smith had accused her of being a CIA officer. They had met and married in India, while his wife was a secretary in the political section of the New Delhi embassy. His wife described his condition as worsening in India due to alcoholism, but Smith reportedly accused her of drugging him. During the testimony at their divorce, which he did not attend obviously, she explained, "he was studying to become a Roman Catholic. He was a Mason; he spoke of joining the fraternal order of the Knights of Pythias." He explained his philosophy "that you had to join these great organizations, even if they were in opposition to each other, just in order to be in with all the big people, you see, so you couldn't be attacked by anyone."[192]

Besides his memoirs, Smith participated in one episode of Peace and Progress radio,[193] a Soviet propaganda radio program, detailing CIA operations in India.[194] After this, Smith's activities have become a mystery. Family members in the US insist there were no communications from Smith, and believe he is now dead.

However, a strange twelve page letter signed by a "J. Smith" appeared in the November

---

[190] Grose, Peter, "U.S. Defector in Moscow is Pictured as a Paranoid in Wife's Testimony in Florida Divorce Case," *New York Times* (December 5, 1967), 12.

[191] Tsang, Steve, "Target Zhou Enlai: The 'Kashmir Princess' Incident of 1955," *China Quarterly* (September 1994), 780.

[192] Grose, "U.S. Defector," 5.

[193] The Peace and Progress Service was a program aired by Radio Moscow during the 1970s.

[194] Rositzke, Harry, *The KGB: The Eyes of Russia* (NY: Doubleday, 1981), 164. Rositzke also wrote *CIA's Secret Operations: Espionage, Counterespionage, and Covert Action* (Reader's Digest, 1977).

1985 issue of *Parapolitics* and several other anti-CIA publications. In the letter, it simply stated, "To whom it may concern, Sincerely, J. Smith, a former CIA officer," and below it was a "List of CIA Agents" of 463 names, years, and the cities they were posted along with the dates of birth.

Of the 463 names listed, 204 were also listed in the anti-CIA database, NameBase,[195] which combined the names of intelligence officers from various anti-CIA publications, US State Department Registers, US newspapers and magazines, US government testimony, and CIA autobiographies. The remaining 259 names can be assumed to also be US government officers, but not necessarily CIA or intelligence. There is also no indication as to whether this was actually "John Discoe Smith" or not. It is unlikely that it was Smith, but more likely a KGB propaganda effort to disrupt CIA operations by listing the names of their agents and areas of operation. The KGB has used this tactic numerous times in the past, and with the fall of the Soviet Union it is unlikely that such lists will appear in the near future.

Incidentally, the identification of active CIA officers and operations is illegal in the United States and punishable by fines and prison terms in accordance with the Intelligence Identities Protection Act of 1982 (PL 97-200).[196]

---

[195] **According to Wikipedia:** NameBase is a web-based cross-indexed database of names that focuses on individuals involved in the international intelligence community, U.S. foreign policy, crime, and business. The focus is on the post-World War II era and on left of center, conspiracy theory, and espionage activities. Founder Daniel Brandt began collecting clippings and citations pertaining to influential people and intelligence agents after becoming a member of the Students for a Democratic Society, an organization which opposed US foreign policy, in the 1970s. With the advent of personal computing, he developed a database which allowed subscribers to access the names of US intelligence agents.

[196] **According to Wikipedia:** The Intelligence Identities Protection Act of 1982 is a U.S. federal law that makes it a federal crime for those with access to classified information, or those who systematically seek to identify and expose covert agents and have reason to believe that it will harm the foreign intelligence activities of the U.S., to intentionally reveal the identity of an agent whom one knows to be in or recently in certain covert roles with a U.S. intelligence agency, unless the U.S. has publicly acknowledged or revealed the relationship.

DOCUMENTS

Approved For Release 2003/03/28 : CIA-RDP80B01676R001600030014-9

Executive Registry
68-104

2 January 1968

MEMORANDUM FOR : Director of Central Intelligence

SUBJECT : <u>I Was a CIA Agent in India</u> by John D. Smith

1. This memorandum is <u>for information only</u> to invite your attention to the attached copy of the Indian Communist Party's publication of <u>I Was a CIA Agent in India</u> by John D. Smith.

2. [redacted] advises me that there is nothing in this booklet which did not appear in the original Soviet articles or on the Soviet radio. Chief, SB Division and CI Staff have also been given copies.

3. If you have no need for retaining this copy, which I thought you would like to see, it would be appreciated if you could return it as there is some demand for it.

/s/

Walter Pforzheimer
Curator
Historical Intelligence Collection

Attachment
  As noted above.

Distribution:
  Orig & 1 - Addressee w/att.
       2 - HIC

B-5

Approved For Release 2003/03/28 : CIA-RDP80B01676R001600030014-9

THAYER ACADEMY
745 Washington Street
Braintree, Massachusetts 02184
(617) 843-3580

April 10, 1992

Mr. Wendell Minnick

Dear Mr. Minnick:

I found the clips on John Smith just after we hung up. He was not a regular student at Thayer, but attended the Veterans School which was a special school set up by the Academy after World War II to assist returning soldiers to earn college entrance credits. He had evidently attended Quincy High School before working at the Fore River Shipyard and joining the Navy, and then took advantage of the opportunity to earn college entrance credits at the Veterans School.

At any rate, Thayer is happy not to claim him! It would be interesting to know what he is doing now and what happened to his family.

I will be most interested to see what you are writing.

Sincerely yours,

Lillian H. Wentworth
Archivist

Wentworth, 100 (1913-2014), also provided additional copies of the local newspaper in her 1992 response to my request for information, including references to Smith's remaining family in the area. I made contact with them and they confirmed they had not heard anything from Smith since his defection.

Name SMITH, John			Room		Class Vet	
	0	1	2	3	4	5	6
MON.					CH	Geom Eng	CHEM ½ yr
TUES.					3	3+	3- C+
WED.					R-	B	Phys ½ yr
THURS.							3 P-
FRI.		VET.TEST	V	525 M 461	Soc. Stud.	587

Aug. 48

3=C

C 13 702 678

Name SMITH, John   Class Vet

Place of Birth Quincy

Date of Birth Month 3 Day 31 Year 26   School last Attended Q.H.S.

Date of entrance to Thayer Academy 6/30/47

Name of Parent or Guardian Mrs. Isabelle Kantola

Home Address: 72 Cranch Street, Quincy, Massachusetts   Phone Pre 2766

Address Business: 1909 - 1907c - 1961
25 hrs. 1909 Amend. 10/8/47

(Over)

Quincy High.

Smith's grades and confirmation of his WW II veteran standing at Thayer, provided by Wentworth. The document suggests that Smith's propaganda tract was actually written by a ghost writer, possibly consolidating his interrogation records into a readable, but factually incorrect, biography.

Defector Says He's Quincy Native

MOSCOW (UPI) — An American who identified himself as a former U.S. intelligence agent said today he defected to the Soviet Union because Washington is preparing "a new world catastrophe."

Quincy Link

The man identified himself as John Smith, a native of Quincy, Mass. He said he once worked for the Central Intelligence Agency in India, but is now a Soviet citizen and lives in Moscow.

Smith told his story in the Soviet newspaper, Literary Gazette, due on the newsstands Wednesday. It was summarized today by the official news agency, Tass.

The American embassy denied all knowledge of the man.

"I never heard of this John Smith," an embassy spokesman said. "The only John Smith I know of was subverted by Pocahontas."

Smith said he spent his first 17 years in Quincy and attended the Thayer Academy in Braintree, Mass. In 1943, he said, he helped build warships at the Fore River Shipyard, then enlisted in the U.S. Navy.

He attended naval academies, then joined the Navy's special liaison department, which deciphered enemy codes. After the war, he said, he entered Washington University.

Smith said he joined the State Department in 1950, was sent to the embassy in New Delhi and recruited by the CIA.

Disillusionment followed, he said. He claimed he began criticizing American policy and was rewarded with "endless checkups of his loyalty, tappings of his private telephone, reading of his letters."

He said he left the State Department and lived in Australia, Africa, Switzerland, Austria and Italy, before deciding to settle "in this great and humanitarian country" and taking Soviet citizenship.

Smith said he was originally entered the State Department even though he "was not very much interested in political questions."

But Tass said that, after he went abroad, "he saw for himself how the U.S. government was suppressing other peoples and how it was engaged in the preparation of a new world catastrophe."

Smith's article appeared tied to two events:

— The 50th anniversary celebrations Nov. 7 of the Bolshevik revolution.

— American claims, denied here, that a Soviet defector named Yevgemy Runge was a Soviet spy.

Smith claimed that "the minds of many Americans are poisoned with propaganda and their eyes sometimes do not want to or cannot see the truth.

"Many Americans just do not want to know the truth, because those who openly cast doubt on the American way of life may get into trouble," he said. "Such persons may be slandered in the press, get letters full of threats, be threatened by telephone. They may be declared 'Reds' or lose their jobs.

"It was intolerable."

Smith said he became a CIA agent because "he sincerely believed that the CIA existed for no other purpose than to take care of American citizens."

But, he said, he discovered the CIA was "engaged in activities dangerous to mankind and absolutely useless to the ordinary American."

When he realized this, he said, he made his feelings known.

The "U.S. Secret Police" began following him, he said. He quit the State Department and began the odyssey that led him to Moscow.

QUINCY — Although there has been no positive identification of the American who has defected to Russia, there is a man named John D. Smith, who was reared in Quincy, and has been a state department career officer.

The Central Intelligence Agency, the State Department or the family of John D. Smith, could not confirm whether there is any connection.

John D. Smith's whereabouts could not be immediately determined. His mother, Mrs. Thomas Kantola of 24 Elliot St., Braintree, said today she had received a letter from him within the week which was mailed in Rome, Italy.

According to a news story published in The Patriot Ledger in 1951, John D. Smith had studied at Quincy schools and Thayer Academy, Braintree, before World War II, when he enlisted in the Navy for a three-year term.

He was attached to the department of state, division of foreign service, after attending George Washington University. In 1951 he was assigned to the American embassy in Pretoria, Union of South Africa.

Mrs. Kantola said today that her son wrote her "he was traveling in Europe." She said her son's wife and children are in this country.

Heard Nothing

Mrs. Kantola said she did not know the nature of her son's work, and did not know whether his tour of Europe was a vacation or a part of his job.

She said she had heard nothing from the state department.

Some in Smith's family heard of the defection on the radio: A cousin, Bryan Donovan of 313 Washington St., Quincy, said that Mr. Smith's work "has always been a kind of secret."

Mr. Donovan said that Mr. Smith had been in the Navy during World War II and returned to college in Washington, D.C. after his release. Mr. Smith had married a school teacher with the embassy department, he said, and has several children.

"The last we heard from him was a letter last Easter," he said. Mr. Donovan said that Mr. Smith had worked with the C.I.A. but was with the American Embassy when he served in India.

Mrs. Duncan MacLeod of Quincy, Mr. Smith's aunt, said that he was at the American Embassy in an African country the last she had heard from him.

Leonard Kantola of 98 Cushing St., Hingham, Smith's half-brother, said he has not heard from him in several years. Mr. Kantola said the last time he heard from him he was with the state department in India.

Smith's step-father is Thomas Kantola a former Quincy police officer.

Leonard Kantola confirmed that his brother had attended Thayer Academy but left to work at Fore River Shipyard during the war years. He said he later left the yard to join the Navy.

In Washington a spokesman for the Central Intelligence Agency said "we never comment on published acounts" although he added "of course we are checking the matter very thoroughly." He said the state department would act as spokesman for the government.

A state department press officer said the matter had been brought to the attention of Robert McCloskey chief press officer for possible future comment later today.

Local article provided by Wentworth.

Appendix I

Colonial Office Statement on the Loss of the Air-India aircraft "Kashmir Princess"

issued on 11 January 1956.

Consequent upon the loss of the Air-India aircraft Kashmir Princess on April 11, 1955 on a flight between Hong Kong and Djakarta, and upon allegations that the crash had been the direct result of an act of sabotage, intensive enquiries were instituted by the Hong Kong Government.

These included the interrogation and enquiry into the antecedents of 71 persons connected in one way or another with the servicing of the aircraft during its stay of just over one hour in Hong Kong.

By mid-May the investigations carried out by the Indonesian Committee of Enquiry, including examination of the wreckage of the aircraft, had led to a strong suspicion that the crash was due to an explosion caused by the detonation of an explosive device lodged inside the starboard wing at the rear outboard corner of the wheelbay. This was confirmed in the Indonesian Government's statement issued on May 27.

Among the 27 persons whose duties took them in the vicinity of the starboard wing of the aircraft and whose activities were consequently under inquiry was Chow Tse Ming, alias Chou Chu, an employee of the Hong Kong Aircraft Engineering Corporation. Direct suspicion did not fall on him until May 18. Enquiries at his address on that day failed to find him and information was subsequently obtained that some hours before these enquiries were made he had stowed away on a Civil Air Transport aircraft and had arrived in Taipei, Formosa, on the same day.

In the course of the subsequent Police investigation of persons who had been associated with Chow Tse Ming before his departure for Formosa, evidence came to light to suggest that he had been procured by persons connected with a Kuomintang Intelligence Organization and had been offered a reward. There was also evidence that on four separate

> 236
>
> occasions subsequent to the crash he had admitted his complicity. The accounts of what he is alleged to have said on each occasion varied slightly in detail, but in general they strongly corroborated each other and contained statements that he admitted that:
>
> (a) he had sabotaged the aircraft,
> (b) he had been promised a reward of HK$600,000,
> (c) he had used a small time-bomb which made a slight ticking noise,
> (d) he intended to stow away to Formosa. In addition there was evidence that shortly before the crash and subsequently until he went to Formosa, Chow Tse Ming spent some hundreds of dollars, a sum well beyond his normal means.
>
> As soon as the warrant was issued the Nationalist Authorities in Formosa were requested to return the man for trial. After repeated reminders they informed Her Majesty's Consul at Tamsui on December 14 that the competent authorities were unable to deal with the matter since the request was not based on legal grounds.
>
> In asking the Nationalist Authorities to hand over Chow Tse Ming for trial, Her Majesty's Government could not, in the absence of an extradition treaty, base their request on legal grounds. They pointed out to the Nationalist Authorities, however, that it was in their own interests that this outrageous crime should be cleared up.
>
> They assured the Nationalist Authorities that Chow Tse Ming would be certain of being justly tried in strict accordance with the laws of Hong Kong and that he would be given every opportunity of presenting his defence.
>
> Despite intensive and continuing investigation, it has not yet proved possible to bring charges against any other persons who may have participated in the crime.

Hong Kong Annual Report 1955, "Colonial Office Statement on the Loss of the Air-India Aircraft 'Kashmir Princess'," Appendix I, South China Morning Post Library (January 11, 1956), 235-36.

| 94TH CONGRESS
2d Session | SENATE | REPORT
No. 94–755 |

SUPPLEMENTARY DETAILED STAFF REPORTS ON FOREIGN AND MILITARY INTELLIGENCE

BOOK IV

FINAL REPORT

OF THE

SELECT COMMITTEE
TO STUDY GOVERNMENTAL OPERATIONS

WITH RESPECT TO

INTELLIGENCE ACTIVITIES
UNITED STATES SENATE

APRIL 23 (under authority of the order of APRIL 14), 1976

U.S. GOVERNMENT PRINTING OFFICE
WASHINGTON : 1976

70-725 O

For sale by the Superintendent of Documents, U.S. Government Printing Office
Washington, D.C. 20402 - Price $1.90

cussion of any double-agent-type activity anyplace."[65] The Deputy Chief of PB/7 also said that he knew "absolutely nothing" about the incident recounted by Hunt.[66]

Pash stated that PB/7 would not have dealt with double-agent problems because his unit was more oriented to planning rather than "operational" activity.[67] Likewise, Pash's Deputy Chief testified that PB/7 never handled double agent problems.[68]

The Director of Operations Planning testified, however, that Pash's unit would have had responsibility for the planning aspects of dealing with a double-agent problem. But the Director was not aware of any specific instances in which the "Special Operations" unit had to handle a double-agent problem. The Director said that assassination or complete isolation was generally regarded as the means of dealing with a suspected double-agent.[69]

C. Assassination Suggestions Rejected by CIA Headquarters

The Deputy Chief of the "Special Operations" unit recounted two instances where assassination was seriously suggested and, in both instances, was quickly and firmly rejected at CIA headquarters.

1. Asian Leader

The Deputy Chief testified that in the summer of 1949, while he was serving as Acting Chief of PB/7 because Boris Pash was out of the country, the Chief of the CIA's political warfare program branch approached him to request the assassination of an Asian leader. After attending a planning meeting at the State Department, the Chief of the political branch—who was the CIA's liaison with the State Department—told Pash's deputy that the Asian leader "must be sent to meet his ancestors." The Deputy Chief of PB/7 testified that the political branch chief assured him that there was "higher authority" for this request.[70]

The Deputy Chief referred the request to OPC Director Frank Wisner's assistant. Soon thereafter Wisner's assistant told the Deputy Chief: "It has gone right to the top, and the answer is no . . . we don't engage in such activities." He instructed the Deputy Chief to

---

[65] *Ibid.* pp. 38, 48–49. Pash also stated: "Mr. Hunt claims to have discussed the alleged assassination matter with me sometime in 1954 and 1955, at least two years after I left the Agency. . . . I categorically deny having had any discussion on any subject whatsoever with Mr. Hunt during those years." (p. 33) Hunt testified that his meeting with Pash could have occurred before 1950 or after 1953—Hunt was on assignment to a non-European nation in the interim—but that it was much more likely that the meeting took place in 1954 or 1955, during which period Hunt was dealing with operations in West Germany. (Hunt, 1/10/76, p. 44–45.) It should be noted that Pash did undertake certain projects in liaison with the CIA after his formal assignment terminated in January 1952.
[66] Deputy Chief, PB/7, 1/5/76, pp. 73–74.
[67] Pash, 1/7/76, pp. 37–38, 48–49.
[68] Deputy Chief, PB/7, 1/5/76, p. 67.
[69] Director of Operations Planning, pp. 27, 34. He testified: "In the international clandestine operations business, it was part of the code that the one and the only remedy for the unfrocked double-agent was to kill him . . . and all double-agents knew that. That was part of the occupational hazard of the job. . . . So in a shadowy sort of a way, we did have in mind that possibly as a last ditch effort [assassination] might come up. But it didn't come up within my time there because we were very slow in getting off the ground on any of these activities." (Director of Operations Planning, 1/12/76, p. 9).
[70] Deputy Chief, PB/7, 1/5/76, pp. 28, 30, 34.

inform anyone involved of this position and to destroy any document related to the incident. The Deputy Chief followed these instructions. The Deputy Chief speculated that Wisner's assistant had been referring to the Director of Central Intelligence when he said that the matter had gone to the "top."[71]

2. East Asian Leader

The Deputy Chief testified that during his tenure at a CIA's station in Asia, where he served after PB/7 was disbanded, he sent a cable to headquarters from the station outlining a proposed media propaganda program. He later learned that the other station officers had attached an additional paragraph to his cable suggesting that an East Asian leader should be assassinated to disrupt an impending Communist conference in 1955.[72]

A reply cable was received immediately from CIA headquarters disapproving the recommendation to assassinate the East Asian leader. According to the Deputy Chief, the cable "strongly censured" the Station and indicated "in the strongest possible language this Agency has never and never will engage in any such activities." The cable added: "immediately proceed to burn all copies" of any documents relating to this request." The Deputy Chief testified that a senior representative from CIA headquarters arrived shortly at the station to reprimand the officers involved in the incident.[73]

III. THE QUESTION OF DISCREDITING ACTION AGAINST JACK ANDERSON

The Washington Post recently reported that, "according to reliable sources," former CIA officer E. Howard Hunt, Jr., "told associates after the Watergate break-in that he was ordered in December, 1971 or January, 1972, to assassinate syndicated columnist Jack Anderson." The *Post* further reported that Hunt had said that the order, which came from a "senior official in the Nixon White House," was "cancelled at the last minute but only after a plan had been devised to make Anderson's death appear accidental."[74]

According to the newspaper article, Hunt's "alleged plan"

> ... involved the use of a poison to be obtained from a former CIA physician, said the sources, who added that the poison was a variety that would leave no trace during a routine medical examination or autopsy.
>
> Hunt told the sources Anderson was to be assassinated because he was publishing sensitive national security information in his daily newspaper column . . .[75]

The Committee staff has found no evidence of a plan to assassinate Jack Anderson. However, a White House effort was made in consultation with a former CIA physician to explore means of drugging Anderson to discredit him by rendering him incoherent before a public

---

[71] Deputy Chief, PB/7, 1/5/76, pp. 35–37.
[72] Ibid., pp. 47–48, 50.
[73] Ibid., pp. 50–51, 56–57.
[74] Washington Post, "Hunt Told Associates of Orders to Kill Jack Anderson," by Bob Woodward, 9/21/75, p. A1, A20.
[75] Ibid., p. 1.

U.S. Senate, Final Report of the Select Committee to Study Governmental Operations With Respect to Intelligence Activities, Supplementary Detailed Staff Reports on Foreign and Military Intelligence. Book 4, *Alleged Assassination Plots Involving Foreign Leaders*, 94th Congress, Second Session, S. Rept. 94-755 (April 23, 1976), 132-133.

Reds Killed Are Intelligence Man And Journalists

Hongkong, April 13 (UP) Chinese Communist journalists in Hongkong this evening confirmed information given to AFP by British officials that among Peiping delegates lost in the crash of the Air India international plane last Sunday was Raymond Huang, former chief of the *New China News Agency* bureau in Hongkong.

Huang was listed in the passenger manifest as Huang Tso-mei, journalist.

Although officially he held the top post in the Communist news agency here Huang actually wielded far greater power than just running the Red news bureau. Official records kept by British authorities here have him tagged as top Communist intelligence operative in this British colony post which he had held since end of the Pacific War.

Huang was educated at Hongkong University, and his pro-Communist activities were known to British intelligence here even before the Pacific War broke out.

British official sources have also identified Li Ping, Shen Chien Tu, Tu Hung, and Ho Feng Ke as correspondents of the *New China News Agency*.

"Reds Killed Are Intelligence Man and Journalists," Taiwan-based *China Post* (April 14, 1955), 1.

BRITISH SHIP CAPTAIN'S VIEW: SURVIVORS AT SINGAPORE

15-4-1955

"U.P.A." and "The Times of India" News Service
SINGAPORE, April 14.

THE British frigate, H.M.S. "Dampier," arrived in Singapore today with three survivors from the crash of the Air-India International Constellation, "Kashmir Princess."

The three survivors—Captain M. C. Dixit, co-pilot, Mr. J. C. Pathak, flight navigator, and Mr. A. S. Karnik, maintenance engineer—were all injured, but were able to walk down the gang plank to waiting ambulances.

According to a "Times of India" News Service message from Bombay, survivors are making satisfactory progress in the naval hospital at Singapore and may return to Bombay on Sunday.

The "Dampier" also brought the bodies of three of the 15 killed in the crash. The bodies were those of the flight engineer, Mr. K. F. D'Cunha, the assistant purser, Mr. J. J. Pimenta, and a third which was unidentified.

Commander Charles Roe, the "Dampier's" skipper, said the plane crashed on its starboard side. He said the scene of the crash was about 340 miles north of Singapore.

He said the three survivors swam with the help of "Mae West" life jackets four miles to Batsu Bilis Island, where they received first aid from the headman of the island. They were then sent to the village of Genting, where fishermen rowed them to the "Dampier."

He said the "Dampier" sent down divers at the invitation of the Indonesian Government. Three bodies came to the surface while the search for survivors was on.

Commander Roe said that an Indonesian launch first found the wreckage. By the time the "Dampier" arrived, three lines had been fastened to the wreck by two other vessels.

He said four divers were sent down, but except for pieces of metal and the three survivors, nothing else was recovered. He said the three survivors were in the water for eight hours before they reached Batu Bilis Island.

Commissioned boatswain, William David Hughes, said the starboard wing of the plane was badly smashed. He said the cockpit was intact, except for a big hole above the navigator's compartment on the starboard side. He did not see the plane's engines and refused to express an opinion

Continued on page 7 col. 2

SURVIVORS WERE IN WATER FOR EIGHT HOURS

Plane Crash

Continued from page 1 col. 3.

on whether the plane crashed in flames.

He said two of the three bodies recovered were found wearing life jackets. He said this indicated that some time elapsed between the discovery of trouble aboard the plane and its crash.

Mr. Hughes said that one of the divers entered the plane's passenger compartment, but found no bodies.

The three survivors were barred from seeing the press and were sent to hospital soon after they landed.

INDONESIAN RESPONSIBILITY

Meanwhile, authorities here said that since the crash occurred in Indonesian territorial waters, it was Indonesia's responsibility to hold an inquiry. They added, however, that if Indonesia asked that an inquiry should be conducted here, that would be done.

A Navy spokesman said that the Royal Navy had turned down a request of the Indonesian Government that the "Dampier" should return on Friday to the scene of the air-crash off Borneo.

Indonesian officials told the Navy that a team of Indonesian air investigation experts would go to the crash scene on Friday and asked that the "Dampier" be there when they arrived.

The Navy spokesman said the Indonesian request had been refused because the frigate had just returned from the area. He said, however, the other Navy ships were still in the area.

Police introduced stringent security checks at Singapore's Kallang airport today on all Indonesia-bound aircraft as a result of the crash of the "Kashmir Princess."

Uniformed police guarded all planes and plainclothes detectives patrolled the air terminal buildings. All passengers' luggage and personal effects were checked before they were allowed to leave the plane and the aircraft were searched after the passengers left.

Meanwhile, Mr. A. E. Clifford, Surveyor of the Air Registration Board in Hong Kong, and Mr. R. S. G. White of Hong Kong's special branch arrived here today to interview the survivors and investigate the crash.

PLANE WAS IN WORKING ORDER
Mr. Vishvanath's View
"U.P.A." & "The Times of India" News Service

SINGAPORE, April 14: Captain K. Vishvanath, Divisional Operations Manager of Air-India International, who has just returned from the scene of the crash, today categorically denied a statement attributed to an Italian passenger, Sgr. Luigi Pirola, that the "Kashmir Princess" was delayed for two hours in Bombay on Sunday.

Captain Vishvanath, in a long during the run-up prior to the take-off.

He said that a "complete, thorough check" was given to the engine concerned and its performance was found to be perfectly satisfactory.

"The flight left for Hong Kong and, being personally responsible for its dispatch, I am in a position to state categorically that the entire flight up to the time of the mishap was uneventful," Capt. Vishvanath said.

"The statement that a furious discussion occurred between the flight crew and the ground engineer is absolutely incorrect," he added. Capt. Vishvanath said that it was "highly improper" of people to make statements without possession of the facts.

SIX MORE BODIES RECOVERED
Singapore Report

SINGAPORE, April 14: The Indonesian Navy today announced that six more bodies, two of them members of the crew, had been recovered from the wreckage of the "Kashmir Princess," bringing the total to nine bodies recovered, in addition to the three survivors.

The announcement added that two Indonesian naval ships were conducting diving operations with a British corvette.

Meanwhile, hopes that more survivors of the crash will be found at sea were growing today, but it was considered possible some of the passengers or crew might have taken refuge on one of the many tropical islands nearby.—U.P.I.-A.F.P. and Reuter.

"Red" Demonstration
"The Times of India" News Service

CALCUTTA, April 14: A Communist-led procession of about 1,000 persons demonstrated in front of the United States Consulate-General here this evening protesting against "the dastardly conspiracy against Mr. Chou En-lai and other delegates to the Bandung conference."

Shouting "Down with the murderers of the Indian pilot" and "Bandung conference zindabad," the procession marched two and a half miles down Chowringhee from Wellington Square to Harrington Street, where the Consulate-General is located.

The demonstrators squatted in front of the premises and demanded that the Consul-General should come out to receive a memorandum. They were informed by the police that the Consul-General was away in Delhi.

Five leaders of the demonstrators later met Mr. E. R. Wilson, Consul, and presented him with a memorandum. Mr. Wilson assured them that he would communicate it to the U. S. Government. The demonstrators then dispersed.

Inquiry Commission

Mr. K. M. Raha, Deputy Director of Civil Aviation Department, and Mr. Y. R. Malhotra, Chief Inspector of Accidents, who have flown to the site of the Air-India International Constellation crash, will visit Hong Kong later to see off-

"British Ship Captain's View: Survivors At Singapore," *Times of India* (April 15, 1955), 1, 7.

"Crash Of Jakarta Bound Plane Seen Engineered by Reds Themselves," Taiwan-based *China Post* (April 15, 1955). Ironically, the reader might note the advertisement on the left side for the CIA's Civil Air Transport (CAT). The same airline that allegedly facilitated Chow's escape from Hong Kong. The airline conducted a thriving business in commercial aviation during the era, partly for concealment and partly to cover exorbitant expenses for covert operations. It was later renamed Air America. See also William Leary's 2002 book, *Perilous Missions: Civil Air Transport and CIA Covert Operations in Asia*.

CHINA POST Tuesday, April 19, 1955. PAGE 3.

Accident Emanated From Extraneous Source, Air India Survivors Opine

Bombay, April 17 (UP) Air India International authorities said today that the three surviving crew members of the ill-fated *Kashmir Princess* were of the opinion that the explosion and fire which caused the loss of the aircraft "emanated from an extraneous source wholly unconnected with the structure of the aircraft."

The explosion and fire were "not caused by failure of any part of the airframe or fuel and other systems in the aircraft," the official statement said.

The statement said "the baggage compartment fire warning light came on, whereupon fire extinguishers were immediately discharged into the compartment, but without effect. An intense fire developed and spread rapidly to the right wing, while the whole interior of the aircraft, including the pilots' cockpit, was filled with thick smoke.

"Captain D. K. Jather decided on an immediate landing on the water owing to the damage to the right wing caused by the rapidly spreading fire, the resultant failure of the hydraulic system and the heavy smoke in the cockpit which destroyed visibility.

"The descent and landing were made under exceptionally difficult conditions. The aircraft touched the water with some force and sank almost immediately. During the rapid descent the air hostess and flight purser secured life jackets to all passengers and crew members and emergency procedures, including opening of the emergency exit, were carried out.

"The aircraft was flying at 13,000 feet in the proximity of Natuna Islands when at about 4.53 local time a muffled explosion was heard and white smoke began to enter the cabin through an air duct.

"Ground engineer Karnik and navigator Pathak were thrown into the sea on the impact, while first officer Dixit escaped through the cockpit's storm window. Dixit and Karnik on one hand and Pathak on the other drifted to separate islands after spending eight hours at sea. They were rescued and brought together by Indonesian islanders at dawn.

"Dixit reports the conduct of all the crew was exemplary, and he makes special mention of air hostess Gloria Berry who, it is feared, lost her life in the crash.

"It is important to note that up to the moment of the explosion and outbreak of fire the aircraft functioned normally in every respect. The right inboard engine, which was nearest the fire, was stopped and feathered by the commander as a precautionary measure during the descent, although it was running perfectly up to the time of ditching.

"The exact cause of the tragedy must, however, be left to be ascertained by an official inquiry after a detailed examination of the wreckage, which lies in relatively shallow waters. Little hope can now be entertained as of the possible survival of any passengers or other crew members."

"Accident Emanated From Extraneous Source, Air India Survivors Opine," Taiwan-based *China Post* (April 19, 1955), 3.

Bandung Dead -- Martyrs Or Satyrs

The recent Air India International plane crash which resulted in the death of a number of Red China delegates to the Bandung Conference has superimposed itself upon the attention of the entire world. Within less than 30 minutes after word of the crash had been dispatched to Communist Chinese headquarters in Peiping, a ringing denunciation of American and Nationalist Government agencies was issued -- declaring that the plane crashed as a result of sabotage upon the part of "secret agents" from these two governments.

Now, from Air India itself, comes the information that the crash was not due to mechanical failure. (See story on page 3) There are other factors which are emerging from the confusion of the first reports which indicate more and more that Communist China herself was responsible for sabotaging the plane and for causing the death of her own personnel, observers here declared.

Before the Communist Chinese will be able to press for world sympathy for the loss of their representatives, the observers noted, they must clarify a number of startling discrepancies which are known to exist.

First, the observers queried, the Red Chinese were known to have expressed their fear of possible sabotage of the planes -- before the even arrived. If this fear were sincere, why didn't they arrange for the planes to be serviced in Canton as in the past. There under complete control of their own personnel there would have been maximum security against the potential risks of providing through Kai Tak Airfield in Hongkong?

Second, the Reds made a clumsy move in having their charges of sabotage ready-prepared. Only 30 minutes after the news was released of the crash, they had issued a list of sabotage charges against the U. S. and Free China. How could it be that a government was able to launch a complete propaganda campaign within moments of information of the disaster? it was questioned.

The Air India confirmation of an extraneous case totally removed from mechanical failure insures the belief of deliberate sabotage. However, it was asked, how could the Chinese Communist regime dare to make such charges cold, prior to an official investigation? How could, be so sure, it was asked, that sabotage rather than mechanical failure was the cause?

They were almost supernaturally aware of facts and events before the rest of the world was even fully acquainted with the preliminary reports of the tragedy, it was noted.

Third, why did the Reds wait four days before sending representatives of their own to the scene of the crash? The observers were concerned that this might have been in a wishful attempt to provide themselves with a clear field to charge obliteration of evidence by the British-Indian investigators while the Communist Chinese were not present.

The observers are interested to know in a penultimate query, if it could be possible that the Red Chinese were willing to "dispose" of a few of their minor functionaries, in an attempt to gain Asian sympathy against U. S. actions during the Bandung Conference? Following a practice well known historically, the Communist Chinese are not averse to elevating a few unwanteds to the rank of "hero first-class", by involuntary martyrdom. Could this be the case now, it was queried? Was it possible that this was intended to mitigate the unsavory taint that the Red Chinese gained through their brutal destruction of the Cathay Airlines plane near Hainan Island last year was the ultimate question?

The observers, surveying the first factual reports from crew members of the ill-fated plane, were willing to bow to the fact of sabotage and deliberate destruction of the plane. The answers they seek, however, were aimed at clearing the atmosphere of a number of unknown quantities which have appeared and which are raising a certain noisome quality to the Communist assertions, condemning the U. S. and Free China.

"Bandung Dead - - Martyrs Or Satyrs," Taiwan-based *China Post* (April 19, 1955), 4.

Air India Crash Caused By Time Bomb, Indonesian Court Of Enquiry Reports

HK GOV'T SEES DEVICE PROBABLY PLACED DURING STOPOVER

New Delhi, May 27 (UP) An official Indonesian court of enquiry said today a time bomb caused the crash of an Air India Constellation that killed Chinese Communist delegates to the Asian-African conference at Bandung.

The court's findings, released today, said the crash of the Air India Constellation *Kashmir Princess* last month was caused by the explosion of an "infernal machine" in the starboard well of the aircraft.

Examination of wreckage dredged from the sea following the crash provided "irrefutable proof" that the plane had been sabotaged, the court said.

The findings of the Indonesian court of enquiry were released early today by the Indian Government.

The constellation plummeted into the South China Sea off the great Natuna Islands April 11 while carrying Red Chinese and Vietnamese delegates to the Bandung Afro-Asian conference. Only three Indian crew members survived.

The court's official statement said the crash was caused "by the explosion of a timed infernal machine in the starboard well of the aircraft".

It said recovery of four parts of a twisted and burned out clockwork mechanism which bore no relation to any part of the plane's equipment provided "irrefutable evidence" that the *Kashmir Princess* had been sabotaged. The clockwork mechanism was trapped inside the wreckage of the plane, it said.

The report said the explosion punctured the plane's number three fuel tank and started an uncontrollable fire. The aircraft was airworthy, properly certified and manned by an experienced crew, the report said.

Indian Premier Jawaharlal Nehru said at the time that the crash had "some very unusual features." But British sources at Hongkong said the chance of sabotage were "extremely remote.

A State Department spokesman in Washington said there was "not a shred of truth" in the Communist charges, which he termed "preposterous." The Chinese Nationalist Foreign Office in Taipei declined comment.

Only hours after the crash the Chinese Communists charged that the plane had been sabotaged by American and Chinese Nationalist agents attempting to "murder" Red Chinese delegates to the Bandung conference.

In Hongkong, the Hongkong Government, which conducted its own investigation independent of the Indonesian enquiry, said it was "probable" that an explosive device had been placed in the aircraft.

A government statement said, however, that a Chinese Communist warning that "something might happen" to the plane, issued before it arrived in Hongkong, did not mention the possibility of sabotage. Security precautions taken during the Hongkong stopover therefore, the statement said, were mainly aimed at preventing possible trouble between the passengers and non-Communist Chinese.

"Had the possibility of sabotage been specifically mentioned," the statement said, "specific action would have been taken for its prevention including a detailed search of the aircraft."

"In view of the time factor it seems most likely that this device was, in fact, placed in the aircraft during its stay in Hongkong," the Hongkong Government said.

"The police have therefore concentrated their questioning on those persons who might be in a position to place such a device in the Indian aircraft. This investigation has been, and still is being pursued with the utmost vigor."

The government statement said it was not in the public interest to reveal the results of the investigation.

[handwritten: CHINA POST MAY 28 1955]

[handwritten: Page 3]

"Air India Crash Caused By Time Bomb, Indonesian Court of Enquiry Reports," Taiwan-based *China Post* (May 28, 1955), 3.

Gov't Says 2 Stowaways Fleeing Red Rule Not Connected With Air Crash

The security authorities here yesterday denied reports that the two stowaways who arrived in Taipei May 19 aboard a CAT plane from Hongkong were connected with the alleged sabotage of an Indian air liner taking Chinese Communist officials and newsmen to the Afro-Asian conference at Bandung.

The two stowaways were arrested for illegal entry to Taiwan without entry permits, the authorities said, adding that they were refugees who fled from the Chinese mainland to Hongkong. The authorities, however, declined to disclose the names of the two persons at the moment.

They were not connected "in any way" with the alleged sabotage of the air liner Kashmir Princess which crashed into the sea off Sarawak April 11 with a loss of 15 lives, the authorities said.

The two stowaways are presently detained for questioning.

Taipei, May 30 (AP) The Government Information Bureau said today that two Chinese Communist cadres who had fled mainland China because they had become disillusioned with the Reds arrived here as stowaways aboard a plane from Hongkong May 19.

The bureau made two points:

(1) The stowaways had nothing to do with the alleged sabotage of the Indian Air Liner Kashmir Princess, which crashed at sea April 11 with a loss of 15 lives while taking Communist officials and newsmen to the Afro-Asian conference at Bandung.

(2) The stowaways were the only persons to have escaped to Taiwan since the crash occurred.

The bureau said the stowaways fled from Red China first to Macao, then to Hongkong.

It attributed their subsequent escape to Taiwan to fear of reprisals by Communist agents in Hongkong.

The bureau disclosed the story in the wake of speculation that the stowaways — originally it was reported there was only one — might have been implicated in planting the time-bomb allegedly responsible for the crash of the Kashmir Princess.

The new stowaways, who were discovered in the baggage compartment of a plane from Hongkong, were said to be still under questioning by the security authorities.

Their identity and other details were not disclosed.

CHINA POST May 31, 1955 Page 4

"Gov't Says 2 Stowaways Fleeing Red Rule Not Connected With Air Crash," Taiwan-based *China Post* (May 31, 1955), 4.

Plane Stowaway From Hongkong Seen Linked To Air India Crash

Police Break Up Student Dancing Parties Given In Private Homes

Police raided two private homes in Taipei on Saturday night and stopped middle school students in both places from continuing with their dancing parties.

The police thinking is that school students should not dance at any event -- regardless of whether at private or public functions. The two parties involved in the closures were a birthday celebration and a farewell party.

Some 40 students of the Cheng Kung Middle School were "cutting a rug" to the music of a phonograph at a birthday party given for a school-mate, Yang Hui-chi, when policeman pounded at the door. They entered, broke up the party and took the names of the teen-age participants. The address of the residence was 90, South You Ping Road.

Another party, given in farewell of Miss Chou Li-chu who is planning advanced study in the United States, was also stopped by police. Some 30 jitterbuggers were "holding a ball" in a private home on North Chungking Road, when the "law" entered and broke it up.

The police revealed that the students belonged to many middle schools including Tamkang English College and the private Chiang Shu Middle School.

None of the students, who were being chaperoned by their elders, were held, nor were there any charges filed, it was reported.

[handwritten: CHINA POST MAY 30, 1955 page 4]

By Spencer Moosa

Taipei, May 29 (AP) Was the mysterious stowaway who arrived in Taipei May 19 in a plane from Hongkong connected with the alleged sabotage of an Indian air liner taking Chinese Communist officials and newsmen to the Afro-Asian conference at Bandung?

The air liner *Kashmir Princess* crashed into the sea off Sarawak April 11 with a loss of 15 lives, and an inquiry by the Indonesian Government attributed the disaster to a time-bomb.

Following the Indonesian verdict, the Hongkong Government said it seemed probable that the explosive device was placed in the aircraft during its stop-over at the British Colony.

Press reports received here today from New Delhi said an Indian newpaper, quoting a "high authority," had said that a Communist Chinese alleged to be implicated in the sabotage had escaped to Taiwan.

The only person publicly known to have "escaped" from Hongkong to Taiwan after the disaster was a man who arrived here May 19 as a stowaway in a Hongkong-Tokyo air liner.

Officials of the company owning the air liner said the man was found hiding in the baggage compartment following the plane's arrival from Hongkong.

He was discovered there by crewmen as baggage belonging to passengers getting off at Taipei was being unloaded

Airport security officials were notified and whisked the man off. The company was not informed of his identity, nor was the press.

In fact, the security authorities have refused to divulge anything whatever about him. The incident was so carefully hushed that it did not break in the newspapers here until a full week later.

The newspapers assumed at the time that the stowaway was probably a Chinese Communist spy who intended to smuggle himself into Taipei for subversive purposes. He might have been, but in view of the reticence of the authorities here it is impossible to tell if he actually was.

The crash of the *Kashmir Princess* was immediately followed by Communist charges that American and Nationalist agents were responsible.

Any Nationalist complicity in the affair was indignantly denied in Taipei, which from the first took the view that some disgruntled Communist might have been responsible.

Moosa, Spencer (AP), "Plane Stowaway From Hongkong Seen Linked to Air India Crash," Taiwan-based *China Post* (May 30, 1955), 4.

HK Police Get Warrant For Arrest Of Aircraft Cleaner For Sabotage

Hongkong, Sept. 3 (UP) The government disclosed today that sabotaging of an Air India plane last April has been solved but one of the saboteurs has fled to Formosa.

Hongkong police applied for and received a warrant in court today for the arrest of Chow Tei-ming on charges of conspiracy to murder in the time bombing of the Indian Constellation *Kashmir Princess* April 11.

Sixteen persons aboard including Chinese Communist diplomats and Red newsmen enroute to the Asian African conference in Indonesia were killed when the plane plunged in flames into the sea off Borneo.

Chow stowed away on a Civil Air Transport plane May 18 and got into Formosa. The Nationalist Government has been asked by the British to retain him but there is no extradition agreement between the two governments.

The official government spokesman here maintained that no evidence of the sabotage having been ordered by the Nationalists has been found.

"There is no evidence that this crime was ordered or directed from Formosa," he said.

Pressed about a possible link to Peiping, he said, "That goes for Peiping too."

The *Kashmir Princess* had been chartered for the Chinese Communist regime to fly 12 newsmen and diplomats to Jakarta. It was on the ground here less than two hours for refuelling before it took off for Indonesia.

But six hours later it plunged into the sea. An official Indian inquiry report said a time bomb planted in the starboard wheel of the plane had caused the plane to crash, killing 16 of the 19 persons aboard.

Chow was a cleaner employed by the Hongkong Aircraft Engineering Corporation, Ltd. He was paid about US$25 monthly. He was on duty and helped clean off the exterior of the *Kashmir Princess*.

Chow and some 250 other persons at Kaitak Airport were questioned during the four month investigation that involved 25,000 man-hours. On May 18 he vanished.

When it was learned a Kaitak employe had stowed away and gone to Formosa, the Nationalist Government said that two Chinese had done so but that both were refugees from the mainland who had simply passed through Hongkong.

Presumably Chow was only one of several persons involved in the sabotage. A government spokesman said, however, that everything points to the plot having been hatched right here in Hongkong.

The spokesman did not comment on the fact that Peiping had cried sabotage hours before the wreckage of the plane had been found. It later was revealed that the Reds had warned that something might happen to their delegates while here but no mention was made of the chance of sabotage.

No Immediate Reaction

Taipei, Sept. 3 (AP) No immediate reaction could be obtained from high Nationalist

CHINA POST (TAIWAN) SEPT 4, 1955, page 1

"HK Police Get Warrant For Arrest Of Aircraft Cleaner For Sabotage," Taiwan-based *China Post* (Sept 4, 1955), 1.

Red Reps Spies In Disguise

By CHINA POST Special Correspondent

Hongkong (Airmailer) Mao Tze-tung's suggestion to the visiting Japanese Diet members this month that he might accept an invitation to visit Japan has caused amused speculation here as to the probable size and composition of the delegation that would probably accompany him (in the extremely remote probability that the Japanese were to invite him).

Informed observers here, at Red China's gateway to the Free World, have collected evidence that the key members of Chinese Communist delegations to non-communist nations, as well as a number of the so-called "advisors" accompanying them, have a long agent and intelligence background. It is common knowledge in intelligence circles that these "delegates", skilled as they are in propaganda work and clandestine contacts, go to unsuspecting foreign countries with a double mission. While selected leaders talk smoothly to prime ministers and their cabinets about "co-existence" and "trade for mutual benefit", these agents propagandize student and labor groups and arrange secure contact through "cutouts" (a "cutout" is a person not subject to suspicion who maintains contact between two agents) with communist agents resident in the host country.

Less Obvious

Aside from such experienced propagandists and agent provocateurs as Chou En-lai; Wang Ping-nar, Chang Wen-t'ien, Wang Chia-hsing, Lei Jen-min and Li Te-ch'uan, there are those whose mission is less obvious.

Take, for example, Liao Cheng-chih. Liao was the key figure in the Red Cross Mission to Japan a year ago. He was an "advisor" at the Geneva Conference in June 1954 and acted in that same capacity at the abortive "Asian Conference For Easing International Tensions" in Delhi last April and the subsequent Afro-Asian Conference at Bandung. Liao has had a checkered career and his background would give even the famed "Sorge" pause. A native of Kwangtung, Liao was born in Japan, where his father was a veteran KMT agent engaged in underground work against the Manchus. He was brought up in Japan by friends of his parents. When he was 11 years old, he returned to China. After graduating from Lingnan University, Liao joined the communist party and carried on recruitment work for them among seamens unions.

Later, he returned to Japan "to complete his education", but was kicked out of the university for engaging in communist propaganda activities. In 1932, he was arrested in Shanghai as a communist agent. Liao then joined the communists in Kiangsi and was later trained at Yenan. He was again arrested, in 1942, at Shao Kwan, the wartime provincial capital of Kwangtung Province. Again, the charge was engaging in subversion for the communists. Chief Secretary of the Communist Youth Corps, Chairman of the "Democratic Youth Association" and Deputy Chief of the Overseas Chinese Affairs Committee, Liao is recognized as the top Chinese Communist agent for Overseas Chinese Affairs. His particular area of interest is Japan, since he spent some one third of his life there.

Shady Character

An even more shady character than friend Liao is Li Ko-nung, Chief of the Red Chinese so-called "Social Affairs Bureau". With their usual penchant for seizing upon the appropriate phrase, the communists have chosen this name for their secret police organization. To them, of course, "Social Affairs Bureau" is most fitting, since the tentacles of the all-powerful Red secret police extend into every club, school, farm and home on the mainland. Li was an "advisor" to the Geneva Conference delegation in 1954 and again at the Bandung conference. Trusted and supported by Mao, Li is chief of all Chinese Communist secret police activities, at home and abroad.

Then there are such colorful characters as Kung P'eng, Yang Chi-ching, Sai Fu-ting, Huang Hua and Fu Hao, all of whom have connections with Red intelligence and propaganda organs.

Yang has been Vice-Minister in the Public Safety Department of the "N. E. Peoples Government" and later Minister of Public Safety in Peiping.

Kung P'eng, a woman, is Chief of the Intelligence Department in the Red Ministry of Foreign Affairs.

Sai Fu-ting, a Uighur tribesman, was picked up by the Bolsheviks many years ago in the Ili Valley area of Central Asia. Adept at intrigue and a willing student, he became a member of the Russian Communist Party when he was 18 years old. He was trained in Moscow and was for a long time a Soviet secret service agent in Central Asia. Last April, he was an "advisor" to the Chinese Communist delegation to the "Asian Conference For Easing International Tensions" at New Delhi. It is significant that he was appointed Governor of the "Sinkiang-Uighur Autonomous Region" recently announced by the Peiping Government.

Communist Agent

Huang Hua became a communist agent upon his graduation from Yenching University in 1936. Rising quickly in the communist party, he entered the Central Political Bureau and was an aide to Yeh Chien-ying during General Marshalls Mission to China. Huang was security chief at the Panmumjon negotiations and later delegation spokesman at Geneva. Although he attended the Bandung Conference ostensibly as Press Chief, he is known to rank high in Chinese Communist intelligence.

As for Fu Hao, an "advisor" to the Red Trade Delegation to Japan last April, his true role was described in the "Keung Sheung Pao" of last March 24th. After discussing the members of the delegation, the "Keung Sheung Pao" goes on the say: "They pretend to be specialists in economics, textiles, electrical engineering and so on ... and go to Japan so that they can do propaganda and political work there. The most obvious ones are: Fu Hao, advisor to this 'delegation', who is an international agent of the Communist Asian Intelligence Bureau. Chen K'ang and Li Sheng-min are top intelligence agents ....".

The story was current in Hongkong, last Winter, that Liao Cheng-chih had been overheard remarking to an aide that he was happy to have found the Japanese journalists so "amai" (naive and easily duped). We do not share Liao's opinion of our Japanese brothers of the fourth estate. With the exception of known communists and a handful of fellow travelers, the Japanese Press is known to be staffed with critical, able and objective reporters. We are sure that they will not be long in unearthing and exposing the double-dealing that lies behind Chinese Communists protestations of good faith.

CHINA POST OCT 28 1955. Page 2

Special Correspondent, "Red Reps Spies in Disguise," Taiwan-based *China Post* (October 28, 1955), 2. Note to reader: this is an exceptional piece of journalism by a "special correspondent," which suggests it was written by either the CIA or a close connector. These are my suspicions, and not based on evidence, but the details of these individuals illustrates an incredible amount of research during the era.

UK Issues Statement On Responsibility Of Air India Plane Crash

Hongkong, Jan. 11 (UP) The British statement charging agents of the Nationalist Chinese Government were responsible for sabotaging an Air India plane carrying Chinese Communist delegates to the Bandung conference last year was released here at the same time it was released in London.

Part of the text reads as follows:

"Among the 27 persons whose duties took them in the vicinity of the starboard wing of the aircraft and whose activities were consequently under inquiry, was Chow Tse-ming, alias Chou Chu, an employee of the Hongkong Aircraft Engineering Corporation.

Direct suspicion did not fall on him until the 18th of May. Enquiries at his address on that day failed to find him and information was subsequently obtained that some hours before these enquiries were made he had stowed away on a Civil Air Transport aircraft and had arrived in Taipei, Formosa, on the same day.

(Continued on Page 4)

Britain Issues
(Continued from Page 1)

"In the course of the subsequent police investigation of persons who had been associated with Chow Tse-ming before his departure for Formosa, evidence came to light to suggest that he had been procured by persons connected with a Kuomintang intelligence organization and had been offered a reward.

"There was also evidence that on four separate occasions subsequent to the crash he had admitted his complicity. The accounts of what he is alleged to have said on each occasion varied slightly in detail but in general they strongly corroborated each other and contained statements that he admitted that:

(A) He had sabotaged the aircraft;
(B) He had been promised a reward of 600,000 Hongkong dollars;
(C) He had used a small time-bomb which made a slight ticking noise;
(D) He intended to stow away to Formosa....."

CHINA POST (TAIWAN) JAN 12, 1956 pages 1/4

"UK Issues Statement On Responsibility Of Air India Plane Crash," Taiwan-based *China Post* (January 12, 1956), 1,4.

港府今晨特別公報

飛機案兇手逃台

港府促解返港訊案

該犯周梓銘在啟德機場工作
四月中行事後五月中逃台灣

1955. 9. 3

【本報消息】港府新聞處今晨九時三十分發表特別公報，指出暗害印航機「喀什米爾公主號」的兇手周梓銘，現已逃往台灣。英國當局已通知台灣當局，將該犯解返歸案。

公報原文如下：「印度航空公司飛機「喀什米爾公主號」於四月十一日失事。經過四個月的週密調查後，香港警方於今晨（星期六）從香港裁判署獲得一逮捕令，逮捕周梓銘（Chow Tse Ming，和Chau Tse Ming），又名周錫鉤（Chau Sik Kui），又名周超（Chou Chu），控告他協同謀殺。他從前受僱於香港飛機工程公司，在印航機停留啓德機場那一天，他是在場參加該飛機的清潔工作的。

「那天下午，『喀什米爾公主號』，在從香港赴雅加達途中，機上發生一次爆炸，之後即墜落海裏。除了三個機上工作人員外，所有機上十九人都已犧牲。

「據悉，周梓銘已於五月十八日早晨乘飛機從香港逃往台灣。爲此，現正要求台灣當局將他解返香港受審。」

Xin News, September 3, 1955

Krishna Menon, *Time*, "India: The Tea-Fed Tiger," February 2, 1962.

BIBLIOGRAPHY

"11 Reds in Air Crash on Way to Parley," *New York Times* (April 12, 1955), 1, 7.

"Accident Emanated From Extraneous Source, Air India Survivors Opine," Taiwan-based *China Post* (April 19, 1955), 3.

"Air Crash Protest by Peking," *London Times* (April 21, 1955); "British Move in Peking," *London Times* (April 28, 1955), 12.

"Air India Crash Caused by Time Bomb, Indonesian Court of Enquiry Reports," Taiwan-based *China Post* (May 28, 1955), 3.

"Air India Statement," Hong Kong-based *South China Morning Post* (April 12, 1955), 1.

"Airliner Bomb Inquiries," *London Times* (May 28, 1955), 6.

"Airworthiness of Ill-Fated Plane Challenged by Pilot Before Flight," Taiwan-based *China Post* (April 15, 1955), 3.

"Bandung Dead – Martyrs or Satyrs," Taiwan-based *China Post* (April 19, 1955), 4.

"Body of Pilot Found," Hong Kong-based *South China Morning Post* (May 3, 1955), 11.

"Bomb in Airliner Wreck," *London Times* (May 27, 1955), 10.

"British Ship Captain's View: Survivors At Singapore," *Times of India* (April 15, 1955), 1, 7.

"Charge Concerning Airliner Resented," Hong Kong-based *South China Morning Post* (April 14, 1955), 1, 18.

"China Sees Sabotage By U.S. In Air Crash," *Times of India* (April 14, 1955), 1.

"Chinese is Accused of Airliner Murders," *New York Times* (September 3, 1955), 2.

"CIA Considered Inducing Death," *Washington Post* (April 2, 1979), A2.

"Crash Arrests Denied," *New York Times* (August 4, 1955), 3.

"Crash of Jakarta Bound Plane Seen Engineered by Reds," Taiwan-based *China Post* (April 15, 1955), 1.

"Crash Report," *London Times* (April 25, 1955), 30.

"Crash Report," *Time* (April 25, 1955), 30.

"Crash Suspects Held," *New York Times* (August 3, 1955), 13.

"Force-Landing By Indian Plane Feared," *Times of India* (April 12, 1955), 1, 7.

"Frenzied Outburst by Red China," Hong Kong-based *South China Morning Post* (April 17, 1955), 1, 8.

"Gov't Says 2 Stowaway Fleeing Red Rule Not Connected With Air Crash," Taiwan-based *China Post* (May 31, 1955), 4.

"H.K. May be Visited For Air Crash Enquiries," Hong Kong-based *South China Morning Post* (April 22, 1955), 1.

"HK Police Get Warrant for Arrest of Aircraft Cleaner for Sabotage," Taiwan-based *China Post* (September 4, 1955), 1.

"Hong Kong Govt. Rules Out Sabotage To Plane," *Times of India* (April 14, 1955), 7.

"Hong Kong Reports No Plane Sabotage," *New York Times* (April 21, 1955), 2.

"India Honors Air Crewmen," *New York Times* (June 19, 1955), 52.

"India Sets Inquiry on Loss of Airliner," *New York Times* (April 15, 1955), 3.

"Indian Plane to be Raised," *New York Times* (April 22, 1955), 15.

"London Disputes Peiping on Crash," *New York Times* (April 18, 1955), 1, 4.

"Memoirs of Former US Spy," *London Times* (November 3, 1967), 4.

"Memoirs of US Secret Agent," *London Times* (October 25, 1967), 4.

"Nationalists Government Disclaims Knowledge," Hong Kong-based *South China Morning Post* (September 5, 1955), 1.

"New Peking Allegation Against H.K.," Hong Kong-based *South China Morning Post* (April 16, 1955), 18.

"Peiping Charges Indian Airliner Sabotage," Taiwan-based *China Post* (April 14, 1955), 3.

"Peiping Vicious Nonsense," *New York Times* (April 15, 1955), 22.

"Plane Crashes Enroute Bandung; Kills 15 Including 8 Peiping Delegates," Taiwan-based *China Post* (April 13, 1955), 1.

"Protest by Britain to China on Plane Crash," Hong Kong-based *South China Morning Post* (April 18, 1955), 1, 18.

"Red Reps Spies In Disguise," Special Correspondent, Taiwan-based *China Post* (October 28, 1955), 2.

"Reds Killed Are Intelligence Man and Journalists," Taiwan-based *China Post* (April 14, 1955), 1.

"Sabotage of Indian Airliner: Definite Information," *London Times* (August 3, 1955), 6.

"Sabotage of Indian Airliner: Formosa's Refusal to Return Suspect," *London Times* (January 11, 1956), 6.

"Search for Airliner," Hong Kong-based *South China Morning Post* (April 12, 1955), 1.

"Slander on U.S.," *London Times* (March 29, 1956), 4.

"Survivor's Story of Air Crash," Hong Kong-based *South China Morning Post* (April 14, 1955), 1, 18.

"Taipei Rebuffs British Request," *New York Times* (September 5, 1955), 2.

"Time Bomb in Airliner," *London Times* (June 13, 1955), 7.

"UK Issues Statement on Responsibility of Air India Plane Crash," Taiwan-based *China Post* (January 12, 1956), 1, 4.

"US Defector Links CIA to '55 Air Crash," *New York Times* (November 22, 1967), 23.

Agee, Philip, *Dirty Work: The CIA in Western Europe* (Lyle Stuart, 1978).

Anderson, Jack, *Peace, War, and Politics: An Eyewitness Account* (Forge, 1999).

Anderson, Raymond, "Russians Say an Ex-CIA Man Who Spied in India Has Defected," *New York Times* (October 25, 1967), 17.

Bearden, Milt, *The Main Enemy: The Inside Story of the CIA's Final Showdown with the KGB* (Random House, 2004).

Bill, James, *The Eagle and the Lion: The Tragedy of American-Iranian Relations* (Yale, 1988).

Burgess, David, *Fighting for Social Justice: The Life Story of David Burgess* (Wayne State University Press, 2000).

Burros, Marian, "CIA Toxin Related to Red Tide," *Washington Post* (September 19, 1975), A21.

Byron, John, and Robert Pack, *The Claws of the Dragon: Kang Sheng - The Evil Genius Behind Mao - And His Legacy of Terror in People's China* (Simon and Schuster, 1992).

Coleman, Peter, *The Liberal Conspiracy: The Congress for Cultural Freedom and the Struggle for the Mind of Postwar Europe* (Free Press, 1989).

Coll, Steve, *Ghost Wars: The Secret History of the CIA, Afghanistan, and bin Laden, from the Soviet Invasion to September 10, 2001* (Penguin Books, 2004).

Copeland, Miles. *The Game Player: Confessions of the CIA's Original Political Operative* (Aurum Press, 1989).

Corn, David, *Blond Ghost: Ted Shackley and the CIA's Crusades* (Simon and Schuster, 1994).

Corson, William R., *Consequences of Failure* (WW Norton, 1973).

Corson, William R., *The New KGB: Engine of Soviet Power* (Morrow, 1985).

Corson, William R., *Widows* (Crown, 1989).

Corson, William R., *The Armies of Ignorance: The Rise of the American Intelligence Empire* (Dial Press, 1977).

Crile, George, *Charlie Wilson's War* (Grove Press, 2003).

Crozier, Brian, *Free Agent: The Unseen War 1941-1991* (HarperCollins, 1993).

De Silva, Peer, *Sub Rosa: The CIA and the Uses of Intelligence* (Times Books, 1978).

De Witte, Ludo, *The Assassination of Lumumba* (Verso, 2002).

Epstein, Edward Jay, *Deception: The Invisible War Between the KGB and the CIA* (Simon and Schuster, 1989).

Evans, Humphrey, *Escape from Red China* (Coward-McCann, 1964).

Evans, Humphrey, *The Adventures of Li Chi a Modern Chinese Legend: In Which a Humble Member of the Working Class Overcomes the Party Establishment* (Dutton, 1967).

Evans, Humphrey, *The Thought Revolution – University Life and Education in Red China* (Coward-McCann, 1967).

Evans, Humphrey, *Thimayya of India: A Soldier's Life* (Lancer, 1960).

Eveland, Wilbur Crane, *Ropes of Sand: America's Failure in the Middle East* (WW Norton, 1980).

Fetherson, Drew, and John Cummings, "CIA Linked to 1971 Swine Virus in Cuba," *Washington Post* (January 9, 1977), A2.

Fischer, Louis, *The God that Failed* (Harper, 1949).

Fischer, Louis, *The Life of Lenin* (Harper and Row, 1964).

Fischer, Louis, *The Life of Mahatma Gandhi* (HarperCollins, 1950).

Fischer, Louis, *The War in Spain* (Nation, 1937).

Gibbs, David, *The Political Economy of Third World Intervention: Mines, Money, and U.S. Policy in the Congo Crisis* (University of Chicago Press, 1991).

Green, Fitzhugh, *American Propaganda Abroad* (Hippocrene, 1988).

Grose, Peter, "US Defector in Moscow is Pictured as a Paranoid in Wife's Testimony in Florida Divorce Case," *New York Times* (December 5, 1967), 12.

Hong Kong Annual Departmental Report by the Director of Civil Aviation for the Financial Year 1955-1956, Section 8, "Aircraft Accidents," Number 62, Page 22.

Hong Kong Annual Report 1955, "Colonial Office Statement on the Loss of the Air-India Aircraft 'Kashmir Princess'," Appendix I, South China Morning Post Library (January 11, 1956), 235-36.

Jackson, Harold, "CIA Chief Who Rescued the Agency from Paranoia," *Guardian* (August 22, 2000).

Kelly, Sean, *America's Tyrant: The CIA and Mobutu of Zaire* (American University Press, 1993).

Kenneth Conboy, *The CIA's Secret War in Tibet* (University of Press of Kansas, 2002).

Leary, William, *Perilous Missions: Civil Air Transport and CIA Covert Operations in Asia* (Smithsonian Institution Press, 2002).

Lelyveld, Joseph, *Great Soul: Mahatma Gandhi and His Struggle With India* (Knopf, 2011).

Lintner, Bertil, *Burma in Revolt: Opium and Insurgency Since 1948* (Silkworm, 1999).

Mader, Julius (Thomas Bergner), *Who's Who in CIA* (1968).

Mader, Julius (Thomas Bergner), *CIA-Operation Hindu Kush* (1988).

Maitra, Nikhil, *Behind the Bamboo Curtain* (1956).

Maitra, Nikhil, *Jawaharlal Nehru: A Biography* (1956).

Maitra, Nikhil, *On the Chinese Communist Government* (1956).

Maitra, Nikhil, *Report on Mao's China* (1954).

Maitra, Nikhil, *The Revolt in Tibet* (1960).

Mangold, Tom, *Cold Warrior: James Jesus Angleton, the CIA's Master Spy Hunter* (Simon and Schuster, 1991).

Marchetti, Victor, and John D. Marks, *The CIA and the Cult of Intelligence* (Laurel Books, 1980).

Marks, John D., *The Search for the "Manchurian Candidate": The CIA and Mind Control* (WW Norton, 1980).

Mathai, M.O., *My Days with Nehru* (Vikas, 1979).

Mathai, M.O., *Reminiscences of the Nehru Age* (Vikas, 1978).

Miles, Milton E., *A Difference Kind of War: The Unknown Guerrilla Forces in World War II China* (Taipei: Caves, 1986).

Moosa, Spencer, "Plane Stowaway From Hong Kong Seen Linked to Air India Crash," Taiwan-based *China Post* (May 30, 1955), 4.

Morgan, Ted, *A Covert Life: Jay Lovestone - Communist, Anti-Communist, and Spymaster* (Random House, 1999).

Peake, Hayden, *The Reader's Guide to Intelligence Periodicals* (NIBC, 1992).

Pisani, Sallie, *The CIA and the Marshall Plan* (University of Press of Kansas, 1991).

Powers, Thomas, *The Man Who Kept the Secrets* (Pocket Books, 1977).

Richardson, Dougall, *U.S. State Department. United States Chiefs of Mission 1778-1973* (US Government Printing Office, 1973).

Ronan, Thomas P., "London Disputes Peiping on Crash," *New York Times* (April 18, 1955), 1, 4.

Rosenthal, A.M., "Chou Aides' Crash Held Due to Bomb," *New York Times* (May 27, 1955), 1, 6.

Rositzke, Harry, *CIA's Secret Operations: Espionage, Counterespionage, and Covert Action* (Reader's Digest, 1977).

Rositzke, Harry, *The KGB: The Eyes of Russia* (Doubleday, 1981).

Smith, Joseph B., *Portrait of a Cold Warrior: Second Thoughts of a Top CIA Agent* (Ballantine, 1981).

Special Correspondent, "Red Reps Spies in Disguise," Taiwan-based *China Post* (October 28, 1955), 2.

Stanglin, Douglas, "The Defector Time Forgot," *US News and World Report* (June 15, 1992), 19.

Survivors of Crashed Indian Plane Picked Up," Hong Kong-based *South China Morning Post* (April 13, 1955), 1, 18.

Szulc, Tad, "Burma Kept Waiting for Arrival of Chou," *New York Times* (April 14, 1955), 1, 10.

Szulc, Tad, "Chou Courts Nasser Before Asia Parley," *New York Times* (April 16, 1955), 1, 3.

Tsang, Steve, "Target Zhou Enlai: The 'Kashmir Princess' Incident of 1955," *China Quarterly* (September 1994), No. 139, 766-782.

U.S. Senate, Final Report of the Select Committee to Study Governmental Operations With Respect to Intelligence Activities, Supplementary Detailed Staff Reports on Foreign and Military Intelligence, Book 4, *Alleged Assassination Plots Involving Foreign Leaders*, 94th Congress, Second Session, S. Rept. 94-755 (April 23, 1976), 132-133. www.intelligence.senate.gov/pdfs94th/94755_IV.pdf

Waller, John, *Beyond the Khyber Pass: The Road to British Disaster in the First Afghan War* (Random House, 1990).

Waller, John, *Gordon of Khartoum: The Saga of a Victorian Hero* (Atheneum Books, 1988).

Waller, John, *The Devil's Doctor: Felix Kersten and the Secret Plot to Turn Himmler Against Hitler* (Wiley, 2002).

Wise, David, *Molehunt: The Secret Search for Traitors that Shattered the CIA* (Random House, 1992).

Wise, David, *Nightmover: How Aldrich Ames Sold the CIA to the KGB for $4.6 Million* (HarperCollins, 1995).

Wise, David, *The Spy Who Got Away* (Random House, 1988).

Woodward, Bob, *Veil: The Secret Wars of the CIA, 1981-1987* (Simon and Schuster, 1988).

Yu, Maochun, *OSS In China: Prelude to Cold War* (Yale: 1996).

INDEX

Acharya 26

Aden 21

affirmative action 14

Afghanistan 4, 5, 10, 15

Africa 5, 17, 25, 28, 31, 35, 36, 40, 55, 64, 67, 68, 69

African Swine Flu 36

Agee, Philip 28

agricultural products 14

Air America 31, 48, 64

Air Force One 43

Air India 17, 18, 30, 31, 32, 33, 34, 36, 37, 38, 40, 41, 42, 43, 44, 45, 46, 47, 48, 56, 57, 62, 63, 64, 65, 66, 67, 68, 69, 70, 73

Air India Skymaster 43

aircraft carrier 3

Albania 45

Ali, Sadiq 24

Allen, George 21

Allgemeiner Deutscher Nachrichtendienst (see East German News Agency)

Alzate, Manuel 15

amai (naïve and easily duped) 72

American University 26

Amman, Jordan 6

Anderson, Jack 29, 60

Anderson, Ralph 3

Anderson, Robert 28

Anti-Castro Terrorists 36

Arabic 21

Argentina 21

Arunachal Pradesh 16

Asia Foundation 31

Asian Conference for Easing International Tensions 71, 72

Asian Leader 59

Assam 16

assassination 21, 27, 31, 32, 33, 35, 36, 59, 60

Associated Press 29, 47

Association for Diplomatic Studies and Training 24

Association of Former Intelligence Officers (AFIO) 5, 8

Athens, Greece 28

atom bomb 42

Attlee, Clement Richard 44

Australia 5, 15, 25, 44, 55

Australia 55

Austria 5, 9, 29, 31, 42, 55

Aviation Liaison Division 22

Babuji 41

Baird, John 48

bandits 43, 44, 64

Bandung Conference 17, 18, 31, 35, 36, 37, 40, 41, 60, 63, 64, 66, 68, 69, 71, 72, 73

Bangladesh 16

Bangladesh Liberation War 16

Bannerjee, General 12, 25

Bates College 6

Bay of Pigs 29

Bay-class frigate 39

Beijing 30, 34, 38, 39, 40, 41, 64, 66, 72

Beijing Radio 41

Beirut, Lebanon 26

Belgian colony 21

Bergner, Thomas (see Mader)

Berry, Gloria 34, 38

Bharatiya Janata Party 28

Bhawanipatna (see Deo)

Bible 17

bicycle accident 10

Bihar 41

Bill 11

blackmail 4, 17, 23

Blee, David Henry 16

Board of Examiners of the Foreign Service 21

Boies, Robert 26

boiler-maker 3

Bolivia 8

Bolshevik Revolution 55, 72

bomb 18, 19, 20, 31, 32, 33, 34, 37, 38, 42, 44, 46, 47, 48, 49, 56, 57, 67, 68, 69, 70, 73

Bombay, India 20, 21, 22, 23, 36, 32, 38, 62

Boner, William 8

Bonn, Germany 21

Borneo 38, 46, 63

Bosun's Pipes 40

brain trust 9

Braintree, Massachusetts 3, 53, 55

brainwashing 5

Brandt, Daniel 50

bribery 29

British Commonwealth 13

British House of Commons 48

British Labour Party 44

Broadcasting Board of Governors 15

Bronze Star 26

Budapest, Hungary 9

Buenos Aires, Argentina 21

bugging equipment 7, 9

Bulgaria 45

Burgess, David 14, 17, 28

Burma (Myanmar) 11, 17, 20, 31, 35, 42, 43

Burns, James 20, 28

Burros, Marian 36

Burrows, Robert 26

Byron, John 43

Cairo, Egypt 22

Calcutta, India 20, 21, 22

Campbell, Walter 21

Canada 14

Canadian High Commission 12, 14

cancer 36

Canton, China 66

car bomb 42

Caribbean Services 29

caste 41

Castro 36

Cathay Airlines 66

Censor Department 21

Central Legislative Assembly 41

Central Political Bureau 72

Ceylon (see also Sri Lanka) 4, 17

Chamar caste member 41

Chandigarh 23

Chandni Chauk 19

Chang Han-fu 35

Chang Wen-tien 71

Chaos, Operation 18

Chapman, A. 17

Charles University in Prague 26

Chau Sik Kui (alias of Chow Tse-ming) 47, 74, 75

Chau Tsz ming (Chow Tse-ming's other spellings of his name) 47, 74, 75

Chavan, Yashwantrao Balwantrao 28

Chemical Branch, CIA 36

Chen Kang 72

Chen Yi 35

Chiang Kai-shek 31, 40, 41, 43

Chief Foreign Purchase Agency 34, 44

China 17, 18, 20, 30, 33, 35, 36, 39, 72

China Post 43, 44, 61, 64, 65, 67, 68, 69, 70, 72, 73

China Quarterly 30, 31, 36, 38, 41, 49

China Radio International 41

China Travel Service (CTS) 38, 42

Chinese Civil War 20, 30, 43

Chinese Communist Party 20, 41, 43

Chinese Cultural Revolution 43

Chinese Nationalists (See Kuomintang)

Chinese Red Cross 41

Chou Chu (Chow Tse-ming alias) 32, 47, 56, 73, 74, 75

Chou Enlai (see Zhou Enlai)

Chow Tse-ming 32, 45, 47, 48, 56, 57, 64, 70, 73, 74, 75

Christianity 14, 17

Chung Pu-yun 34

Church Committee 36

church services 17

CIA Inspector General 5

Cipher Operation 20

Cipher Section 3

Civil Air Transport (CAT) 31, 33, 47, 48, 56, 64, 68, 70, 73

Civil Aviation Department 46

Clifford, A.E. 63

coal miners 14

coconut plantation 38

codes 3, 4, 5, 6, 7, 8, 18, 20, 48, 55

coffins 39, 40

Cogan, Charles 15, 25

Colby, William 18

Cold War 4, 22, 43, 48

Coleman, Peter 22

Columbia University 28

Communist Party of India 2, 48

Communist Youth Corps 71

Conboy, Kenneth 28

Congo (see also Zaire) 15, 21

Congress for Cultural Freedom 22

Congress of Industrial Organizations 14

conspiracy 44, 50

Constellation Aircraft 37, 43, 46, 62, 67

Constituent Assembly of India 41

Cooperative farm societies 14

Cooperative Union of the USA 14

Corson, William 32, 36

Costa Rica 28

counterinsurgency 32

Counterspy 11

Crozier, Brian 22

Cuba 29, 36

Cunha, K.D. 34, 40, 62

Curran, Jack 11, 13, 15, 19, 20, 25, 33

Current 23

Curtis 12

Czechoslovakia 26, 45

Dacca, Bangladesh 16, 17

Dai Li (Tai Li) 43

Dampier, HMS 39, 40, 46, 62, 63, 64

dark room No. 2 8

Daryaganj Market 19

database 50

de Silva, Peer 42

defection 2, 33, 53, 55

Delhi Gate 19

democracy 20, 28, 44

Democratic Youth Association 71

Deo, Pratap Keshari (Bhawanipatna) 23

Dhaka (see also Dacca) 16

Dikshit 18

diplomatic license plate 9, 26

Directorate of Operations, CIA 15

disease 36

Distinguished Intelligence Medal 5

divers 39, 62

divorce 49

Dixit, M.C. 34, 38, 39, 62, 64, 65,

dog 33

Don Juan 15

Donovan, Bryan 55

Dorrey, Frank 21

Douglas C-54 43

drugs 49

Dulles, Allen 11, 28, 32, 36

East Asian Leader 32, 35, 36, 60

East European Division, CIA 42

East German News Agency 34, 44

East Germany 6, 45

Eastern Europe 18, 26, 31, 42

Eastern India News Agency 22

Eastern Pakistan 16

Eastern States Union 23

Egypt 8, 22, 37, 39, 42

Eisenhower, Dwight 32, 36

elections 25, 26, 27, 28, 76

electronic guard 6

energy diplomacy 22

environmentalist 26

Europe 5, 15, 17, 22, 39, 55

Evans, Humphrey 11

extradition 33, 47, 57

Far Eastern Economic Review 30

farm cooperatives 28

Farmers Union 14

Farmers' Educational and Cooperative Union of America 14

fascist 26, 33, 44

Faxon, Mr. 3

Federal Bureau of Investigation (FBI) 21, 22

Felder, Alex 14

Fifth Column, The 44

Fighting for Social Justice 14

Fiji 32, 45

Finnish extraction 3

Fischer, Louis 23

five principles of coexistence 35

Flanagan, John 21

flying boats 39

For Whom the Bell Tolls 44

Ford automobile 9

Fore River Shipyard 3, 53, 55

Formosa (see Taiwan)

fourth estate 72

France 33, 35

Franco, Francisco 44

Frankfurt, Germany 32

freighter 39

French language 8, 21

French tobacco 19

frigate 39

Fu Hao 72

Galbraith, John Kenneth 25

Ganatantra Parishad Kalahandi 23

Gandhi, Mahatma 23, 26, 27

Gandhian Socialist 26

Gao Gang 43

Garuda Indonesian Airways 46

General Dynamics Corporation 3

General German News Service 44

Geneva Conference 30, 71

Geneva, Switzerland 72

Gentner, Leo 24

George Mason University 26

George Washington University 3, 18, 55

George Washington's Sino-Soviet Institute 18

Georgia 14

German 21, 44

Germany 21, 32, 35, 36, 44, 45

Ghandi, Indira 27

Ghosh, Amar 22

Ghosh, Atul Krishna 22

ghost writer 54

God 17

graft 15

Grantham, Alexander 32, 45

Greece 28

Grimsley, William 28

Grover, John 16

Guangdong Province 42, 43

Guatemala 32

guerillas 16, 43

Gurgaon Road 9

Hainan Island 66

Hamburg, Germany 21

Hamilton, Victor 2

Hankow, China 34, 45

Hao Feng-ke 34, 44

Harvard University 15, 21

Haryana, India 9, 23

Hawaii 24

heart attack 36

Hemingway, Ernest 44

hero first-class 66

Himachal Pradesh, India 12

Hindali 2

Hindi 10, 22

Hindu Kush 29

Hindu nationalists 27

Hindu right-wing organization 28

Hindustan Standard 22

Historical Intelligence Collection, CIA 52

Ho Feng Ke 61

Homage to Catalonia 44

Hong Kong 3, 17, 19, 20, 30, 31, 32, 38, 39, 40, 41, 42, 43, 44, 45, 46, 47, 48, 56, 57, 61, 63, 64, 66, 68, 69, 70, 71, 73

Hong Kong Aircraft Engineering Corporation 32, 47, 56, 70, 73

Hong Kong Group 32

Hong Kong police 33, 38, 46, 70

Hong Kong University 45, 61

Honolulu 15, 24

Huang Chen 35

Huang Hua 72

Huang Tso-mei (Raymond Huang) 45, 61

Hughes, William David 62, 63

Hung Tso-mei 34, 44

Hungary 9, 45

Hunt, E. Howard 59, 60

Ili Valley 72

Imphal 16

India's Gallantry Award 40

Indian Air Force Base 9

Indian Communist Party 52

Indian Council of States 16

Indian counter-intelligence 10

Indian Express 22, 23

Indian Investigation Bureau 28

Indian military 10, 11, 12, 13, 15, 16, 17, 25

Indian National Congress 24, 26, 27, 28

Indian police 7, 22

Indonesia 14, 17, 18, 20, 31, 35, 37, 38, 39, 40, 45, 46, 63, 64, 65, 67, 69, 70

Indonesian Air Force 39, 46

Indonesian Board of Enquiry 32, 45, 56, 67

Inner Mongolia 34, 45

insurgency 20

Intelligence Identities Protection Act (PL 97-200) 50

Iran 5, 21, 32

Iraq 39

Italy 5, 21, 26, 28, 33, 55, 63

Izvestia 2

Jackson, Harold 16

Jain Temple 19

Jakarta (Djakarta) 17, 28, 31, 37, 43, 56, 64

Jan Sangh Party 28

Janata Party 28

Japan 3, 6, 28, 35, 41, 69, 71, 72

Japanese code 6

Japanese destroyer 3

Japanese Diet 71

Jatar, D.K. 18, 34, 37, 38, 40, 65

Jensen, Friedrich 34, 44, 45

Johnson, Lyndon 18

Jordan 6

journalists 11, 17, 22, 23, 27, 29, 31, 34, 37, 38, 40, 44, 45, 72

junk (boat) 19

Kabul, Afghanistan 10, 28

Kai Tak Airport 38, 42, 47, 66, 70

Kamalnayan 23

Kamaraj, Kumarasami 27

Kamikaze Dog

Kang Sheng 43

Kantola, Isabelle 54

Kantola, Leonard 55

Kantola, Thomas 3, 55

Kao Kang 64

Karachi, Pakistan 8, 22, 28

Karaka 23

Karnik, Anant Shridar 17, 18, 34, 38, 29, 62, 64, 65

Kashmir State Assembly 24

Kathmandu 28

Kaufman 6, 7

Keen, Thomas 14

Kelly (dog) 33

Kersten, Felix 5

Keung Sheung Pao 72

KGB 2, 16, 18, 20, 32, 50

Khartoum 15, 28

Kiangsi 71

kidnapping 36

Knights of Pythias 49

Knox 28

Komitet Gosudarstvennoi Bezopanosti (see KGB)

Kong Hoi-ping 32

Konstantinov, Ingvar 2

Korean War 30, 43, 44

Kowloon, Hong Kong 38

Kripalani, J.B. (Acharya) 26

Kuching, Sarawak 37

Kung Peng 72

Kunha, K.D. 64

Kunming, China 42

Kuomintang (KMT) 20, 30, 31, 32, 33, 35, 36, 39, 40, 41, 42, 43, 44, 46, 47, 49, 56, 57, 64, 66, 67, 70, 71, 73

Kuomintang Security Bureau 32

Kuwait 6

Kwangtung Province 71

Laos 26

Leader of the Common People 28

Leary, William 31, 47, 64

Lebanon 26

Lee, Robert 21

Lei Jen-min 71

Lelyveld, Joseph 27

Lenin 23

Leopoldville 15

Li Chao-chi 34, 45

Li Chi 11

Li Ko-nung 71

Li Ping 34, 44, 61

Li Sheng-min 72

Li Te-chuan 41, 42, 71

Liao Cheng-chih 71, 72

Libya 2

Lima, Peru 21

Lin Biao 43

Lingnan University 71

Lintner, Bertil 20

Literaturnaya Gazeta 2, 33, 48, 55

Llanten 19

Lloyd, Selwyn 48

Lockheed 37

Lok Sabha 41

London 73

Los Alamos 42

Lucknow 25

Lumumba 21

Lund, John 15, 21

Lundtsien Tea 19

Luppi, Hobart 22

Macaller, Joseph 16

Macao 48, 68

MacLeod, Duncan 55

Mader, Julius (Thomas Bergner) 6, 8, 9, 21, 28, 29

Madras, India 20, 21

Maharaja of Kalahandi 23

Maharajah of Orissa 23

Maharajahs 23, 24

Maharashtra 28

Maidens Hotel 19, 20, 33

Maihotra, Y.R. 63

Maitra, Nikhil 22

Manchuria 43, 64

Manchurian Candidate 28

Manchurian episode 64

Manchus 71

Manipur 16

Mansfield, Mike 41

Mao Zedong (Mao Tse-tung) 23, 35, 43, 71

Marchetti, Victor 4

Marelius, Edward 9, 28

Marks, John D. 4, 6, 7, 28

Marshall Mission 21, 43, 64, 72

Marshall, George C. 43

martial law 20

martyr 66

Masani, Minocher Rustom (Minoo) 24

Mason 49

Massachusetts 2, 3, 53, 54, 55

Mathai, M.O. 15

Mavalankar, Ganesh Vasudev 41

McCloskey, Robert 55

Menon, K.K. 39

Menon, Krishna 24, 25, 26, 76

mental illness 2

Mick 10

Middle East 2, 21

migrant workers 14

Miles, Milton 43

military intelligence 4, 13, 14, 28, 32, 35, 36, 43, 60, 82

Milks, Harold 28, 29

mind control 28

Mingaladon Airport 43

miniature camera 7

Minister of Internal Affairs 27

Minister of Public Safety 72

Minoo 24

misinformation 17

Misra 22

MK-3 timer 32, 49

Mobutu 21

Moiz 6, 7, 8

Mongolia 43 (see also Inner Mongolia)

Montana 41

Montevideo 21

Moosa, Spencer 47, 69

Moraes, Francis Robert 23

Moroccan Embassy 8

Morocco 6, 8, 15, 18, 49

Moscow 2, 29, 55, 72

Mumbai (see Bombay)

Munich, Germany 18

murder 17, 29, 31, 40, 63, 67, 70

Myanmar 16, 20, 37 (see also Burma)

mystic 26

N.E. People's Government 72

Naga Tribesmen 16

Nagaland 16, 17

NameBase 50

Nanda, Gulzarilal 27

Nasser, Gamal Abdel 37, 42

National Civil Service Award 5

National Farmers Union 14

National Reporter 11

National Security Agency (see US National Security Agency)

Natuna Islands 31, 37, 65, 67

Nazi Germany 44

Near East Division, CIA 15

Needham, Thomas 21

Nehru, Jawaharlal 11, 15, 23, 24, 25, 27, 31, 37, 42, 46, 67, 76

Nehru's Evil Genius 24, 76

Nepal 20, 21, 28

Neues Deutschland 44

New China News Agency 61

New China News Agency (Xinhua) 34, 38, 40, 42, 44, 45, 61

New Delhi, India 5, 6, 8, 9, 10, 11, 12, 15, 17, 18, 19, 20, 21, 22, 26, 27, 28, 49, 55, 63, 71, 72

New Jersey 14

New York 2, 18

New York Times 27, 28, 41

Newark, New Jersey 14

Newport, Rhode Island 3

Nicaragua 8

Nixon, Richard 12, 18, 30

non-aggression 35

non-governmental organization 27

North Atlantic Treaty Organization (NATO) 45

North Korea 44

North Vietnam 31

Nueva Ecijia Province 15

Number Five Liaison Group 32

Oberlin College 14

Odisha 22

Office of Strategic Services (see also Veterans of OSS and OSS Society) 5, 11, 16, 18, 43

Okinawa 26

Old Delhi 19

Operation Chaos 18

Operation Lighter 5, 6, 7

opium trade 20

Orissa 23

Oriya language 22

Orwell, George 44

OSS Society (see also Veterans of OSS and the Office of Strategic Services) 5

Overseas Chinese Affairs Committee 71

Oxford University 30, 32

pacificism 14

Pack, Robert 43

Pakistan 4, 8, 15, 16, 17, 28

Panmunjon talks 72

Pappas, Clara 16

Parakal, Pauly V. 16, 26

paranoia 2, 16, 49

paranoid schizophrenia 2

Parapolitics 50

Paris, France 15, 28, 33

Pash, Boris 36, 59

Patak, J.C. 18, 34, 38, 39, 62, 64, 65

Patriot Ledger 55

PB/7 (see Program Branch 7)

Peace and Progress Radio 18, 49

Peace Corps 14, 28

Peking (see Beijing)

Peleliu 26

People's Guardian 23

persona non grata (PNG) 25

Peru 21

Peterson, Barbara 10

Peterson, Peter 9

Pforzheimer, Walter 52

Philippines 3, 15, 39

phone tapping 4, 10

Pike 14, 15

Pimenta, J.J. 34, 38, 40, 62, 64

Plantain 19

Plutarch 13

Pocahontas 55

poems 44

poison 32, 36, 43

Poland 31, 34, 44, 45

police 4, 7, 20, 22, 33, 38, 46, 56, 70, 71

police dog 33

political warfare 59

Pontianak, West Borneo 46

Portuguese 21

Pradeep 22

Prague, Czechoslovakia 26

Prasad, Rajendra 40

Pravda 33, 48

pregnancy 10

Pretoria, South Africa 55

Price Control Board 24

Princess of Kashmir (see Air India)

Program Branch 7 (PB/7) 35, 36, 59, 60

propaganda 6, 21, 28, 35, 45, 49, 54, 55, 64, 66, 71

provocation 24

psychiatrist 49

Public Safety Department 72

Punjab 23

Purple Heart 26

Quantico National Cemetery 8

Quincy High School 3, 53, 54

Quincy, Massachusetts 2, 3, 53, 54, 55

Rabat 15

Radio Free Europe 15

Radio Moscow 49

Raha, K.M. 63

Raj 14

Rajasthan 16

Ralph 13

Ram, Jagjivan (Babuji) 41

Ranga, N.G. 24

Rangoon, Burma 31, 37, 42, 43

Rape of Tibet 22

Rashtriya Swayamsevak Sangh (RSS) Party 27, 28

Red Cross 41, 71

Republic of China 26

Revolt in Tibet 23

Rhode Island 3

River Trading Post 19

Roe, Charles 39, 46, 62

Roman Catholic 49

Romania 45

Rome, Italy 5, 13, 26, 28, 55

Ronson lighter 7

Rositzke, Harry 18, 20, 25

Royal Navy Survey Ship 39

RSS (see Rashtriya Swayamsevak Sangh)

Runge, Yevgemy 55

Russell, Seymour 28

Russia 2, 18, 20, 43, 72

Russian Communist Party 72

sabotage 17, 18, 32, 40, 41, 43, 46, 47, 56, 64, 66, 67, 69, 70, 73

Sai Fu-ting 72

Saigon, South Vietnam 42

sandalwood fan 19

Sarawak 37, 69

satyr 66

Saudi Arabia 4

Schlesinger, Arthur M. 26

Scotch Whisky 12

Sedman, Leonard 26

Sen, Colonel 25

Seoul, South Korea 42

Shahjahanabad 19

Shanghai 71

Shannon, Charles 21

Shao Kwan 71

sharecroppers 14

Shastri, Lal Bahadur 27

shellfish 36

Shen Chien-tu 34, 44, 61

Sherman, William 24

Shih Chih-ang 34, 44

Shook, Pat 11

Shri Digambar Jain Lal Mandir 19

Sidanau Island 39

Sikh 11

Silver Ash 39

Silver Street 19

Simla 12

Singapore 18, 39, 40, 41, 43, 46, 62, 63, 64

Singh, Jogendra 23

Singh, Ram Subhag 22, 24

Sinkiang-Uyghur Autonomous Zone 72

Skymaster aircraft 43

slander 17, 24, 48, 55

Smith, Glenn Leigh 21, 22

Smith, Joseph 22, 31, 42,

Smith, Mary London (wife) 4, 5, 10, 11, 12, 13, 14, 20, 49

snake charmer 24, 76

Social Affairs Bureau 71

social democracy 28

social justice 14

socialist 26, 44

Socialist Unity Party 44

sociology 11

Sorge 71

South Africa 4, 5, 16, 55

South Asia Division, CIA 15

South China Sea 64, 67

Southern Tenant Farmers Union 14

Souza, D. 34, 38

Sovereignty 35

Soviet Bloc 6, 49

Soviet Division, CIA 18

Soviet Union 2, 5, 6, 15, 17, 18, 33, 39, 44, 45, 48, 49, 55, 72

Spain 21, 23

Spanish 21

Spanish Civil War 44

Special Branch of Hong Kong Police 38

Special Consultant to the United States Commissioner 32

Special Correspondent 71, 72

Sri Lanka (see also Ceylon) 6, 17

St. George's Cross 40

Stanglin, Douglas 2

Starec, Jeremi 34, 44, 45

State Department (see US State Department)

State of Orissa 22

Stern, Thomas 24

Stillwell, Miss 26

Students for a Democratic Society 50

Sudan 5, 15, 28

suicide 43

Sunderland Flying Boats 39

surgeon 44

Swatantra Party 24, 28

Sweden 9, 28

Swedish coding machine 8

Switzerland 5, 33, 55

Syria 21

Szulc, Tad 35, 41, 43

Taipei, Taiwan 47, 48, 56, 67, 68, 73

Taiwan 26, 30, 32, 33, 36, 42, 44, 45, 46, 47, 48, 56, 57, 61, 64, 65, 67, 68, 69, 70, 72, 73

Tamil Nadu 27

Tamsui, Taiwan 57

Tass 55

Taype trawler 39

Tea-Fed Tiger 76

Technical Cooperation Mission 16

Technical Services Division, CIA 28

Tentent Village 39

territorial integrity 35

terrorists 36

Thailand 26

Thayer Academy 3, 53, 55

Thimmaya, Kodendera Subayya 11, 12, 25

Third World 17, 21

Thought 22

Tibet 18, 29

Ticonderoga (CV-14) 3

Timberlake 21

Time magazine 24, 25, 76

Times of India 41, 46

Tokyo, Japan 69

Toronto, Canada 21

toxins 36

Trevelyan, Humphrey 39, 40

Trieste, Italy 28

Truscott, Lucien 32, 36

Tsang Yat-nin 32

Tsang, Steve 30, 31, 36, 38, 41, 47, 49

Tse Hung 34

Tu Hung 61

Turkey 21

U Nu 31, 37, 42

Unger, Leonard Seidman 26

Union Flag 40

United Nations 2, 14, 24

United Nations Children's Fund 14

University of California 22

University of Oklahoma 22

untouchables 41

US Arms Control and Disarmament Agency 21

US Army 6, 15, 26, 28, 42, 43

US Army Air Force 43

US Coast Guard 39

US Department of Defense (DoD) 15

US House of Representatives 41

US Information Agency (USIA) 15

US Information Service (USIS) 15, 20, 21, 22, 23, 24

US Marine Corp 26, 32, 36

US National Security Agency 2

US Navy 3, 9, 28, 55

US Office of Price Administration 24

US Senate Committee 32, 35, 41, 58, 60

US Senate Foreign Relations Committee 41

US Senate International Operations Report 33

US State Department 2, 3, 4, 6, 8, 9, 15, 18,

20, 21, 22, 26, 28, 41, 48, 49, 50, 55, 59, 67

Uttar Pradesh, India 25

Uyghur 72

Van Fen (see Wang Feng)

Veterans of OSS (see also OSS Society and the Office of Strategic Services) 16

Veterans School 3, 53

Vienna, Austria 9, 29, 42

Vietminh 34, 38

Vietnam 17, 20, 31, 32, 38, 42, 67

Vigo 21

Violence in Tibet 22

Vishwanath, K. 39, 63

Voice of America 15

Vuong Minh Phuomg 34

Waller, John 5, 6, 7

Wang Chia-hsing 71

Wang Feng (Van Fen) 19, 20, 33

Wang Ping-nar 71

Warsaw Pact 44, 45

Washington, DC 2, 3, 6, 13, 16, 18, 24, 55

Watkinson 26

Wentworth, Lillian H. 53, 54

West Borneo 46

West Germany 36

Weymouth Fore River 3

Whampoa Military Academy 43

white ensign 40

Who's Who in CIA 6, 8, 9, 21, 28, 29

Wilson, E.R. 63

Wisner, Frank 59, 60

Woodward, Bob 15

World War II 3, 5, 8, 11, 26, 36, 42, 43, 45, 50, 53, 54, 55, 61

World Youth Assembly 26

Wu Yi-chin 32

Xin News 74, 75

Xinhua (see New China News Agency)

Yale University 26

Yang Chi-ching 72

Yeh Chi-chuang 35

Yeh Chien-ying 72

Yenan 71

Yenching University 72

Yu Pui 47

Yu, Maochun 43

Yugoslavia 21

Zaire 21

Zhou Enlai 18, 30, 31, 32, 33, 34, 35, 36, 37, 38, 39, 40, 42, 43, 44, 45, 63, 64, 71

Zippo lighters 7

Zurich 21

Made in the USA
Columbia, SC
26 June 2021